DATE DUE

CORINNE MAIER · ANNE SIMON

EINSTEIN

AN ILLUSTRATED BIOGRAPHY

NOBROW

LONDON – NEW YORK

Thank you to Christophe Vignat
for his precious advice.

FSC
www.fsc.org

MIX
Paper from
responsible sources
FSC® C002795

Einstein © DARGAUD 2015, by Simon, Maier
www.dargaud.com
This is a first English edition published in 2016 by Nobrow Ltd.
62 Great Eastern Street, London, EC2A 3QR.
Corinne Maier and Anne Simon have asserted their right under the Copyright,
Designs and Patents Act, 1988, to be identified as the author and illustrator of this Work.
Translated by Etienne Gilfillan and Arran Brown.

Published in the US by Nobrow (US) inc.
Printed in Latvia on FSC assured paper.
ISBN: 978-1-910620-01-4
Order from www.nobrow.net

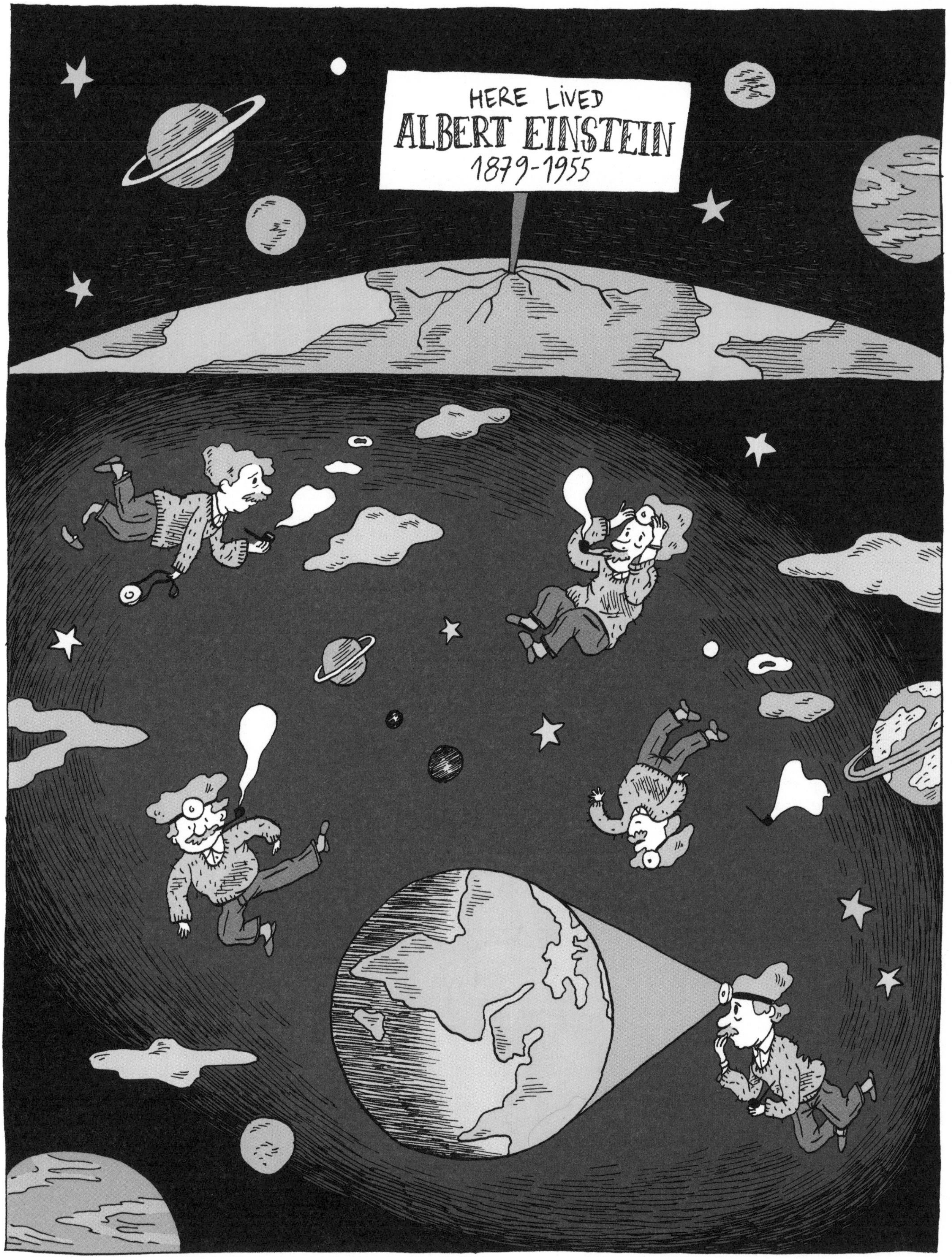
HERE LIVED
ALBERT EINSTEIN
1879-1955

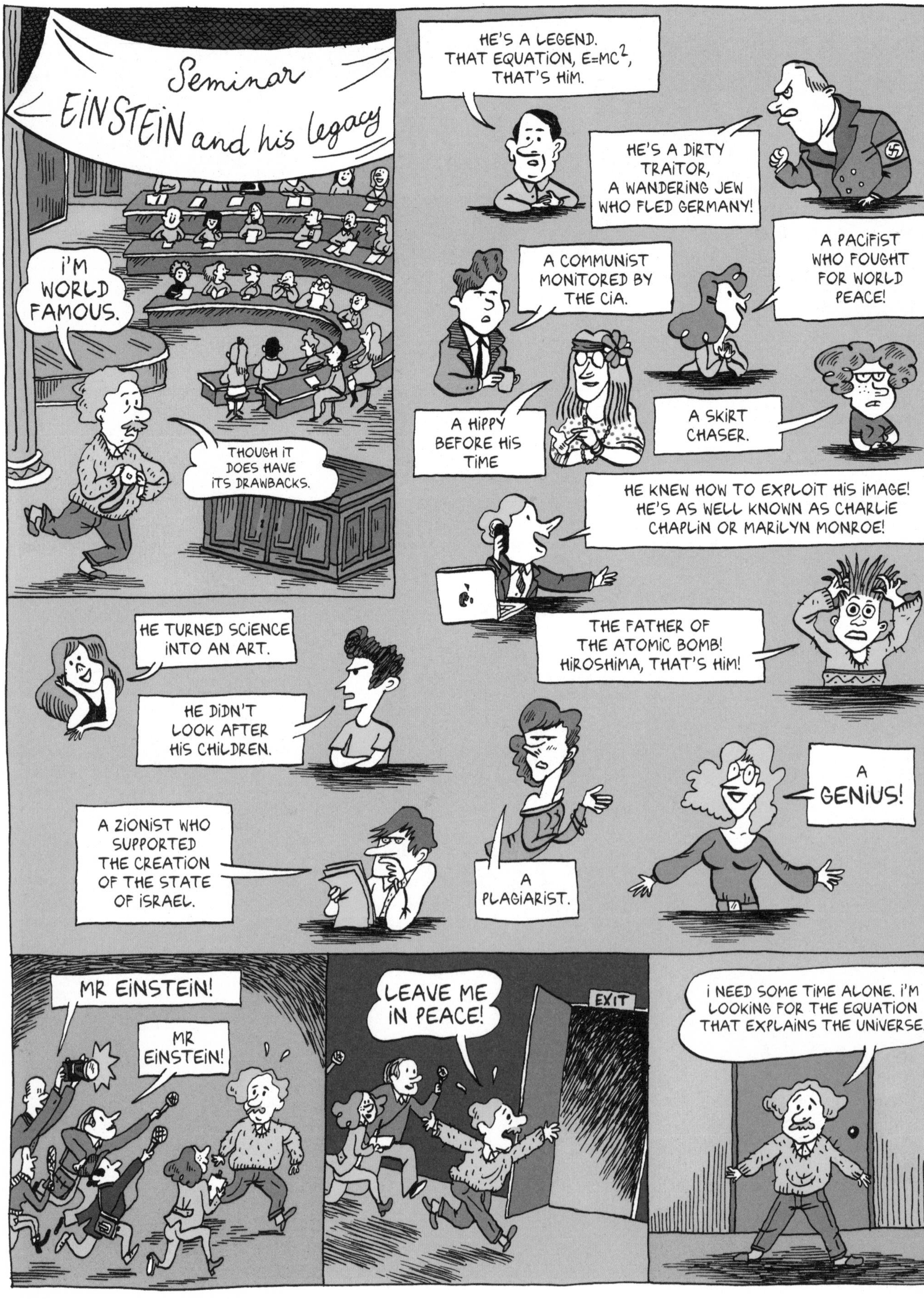
Seminar
EINSTEIN and his legacy
I'M WORLD FAMOUS.
THOUGH IT DOES HAVE ITS DRAWBACKS.
HE'S A LEGEND. THAT EQUATION, $E=MC^2$, THAT'S HIM.
HE'S A DIRTY TRAITOR, A WANDERING JEW WHO FLED GERMANY!
A COMMUNIST MONITORED BY THE CIA.
A PACIFIST WHO FOUGHT FOR WORLD PEACE!
A HIPPY BEFORE HIS TIME
A SKIRT CHASER.
HE KNEW HOW TO EXPLOIT HIS IMAGE! HE'S AS WELL KNOWN AS CHARLIE CHAPLIN OR MARILYN MONROE!
HE TURNED SCIENCE INTO AN ART.
HE DIDN'T LOOK AFTER HIS CHILDREN.
THE FATHER OF THE ATOMIC BOMB! HIROSHIMA, THAT'S HIM!
A ZIONIST WHO SUPPORTED THE CREATION OF THE STATE OF ISRAEL.
A PLAGIARIST.
A GENIUS!
MR EINSTEIN!
MR EINSTEIN!
LEAVE ME IN PEACE!
EXIT
I NEED SOME TIME ALONE. I'M LOOKING FOR THE EQUATION THAT EXPLAINS THE UNIVERSE.

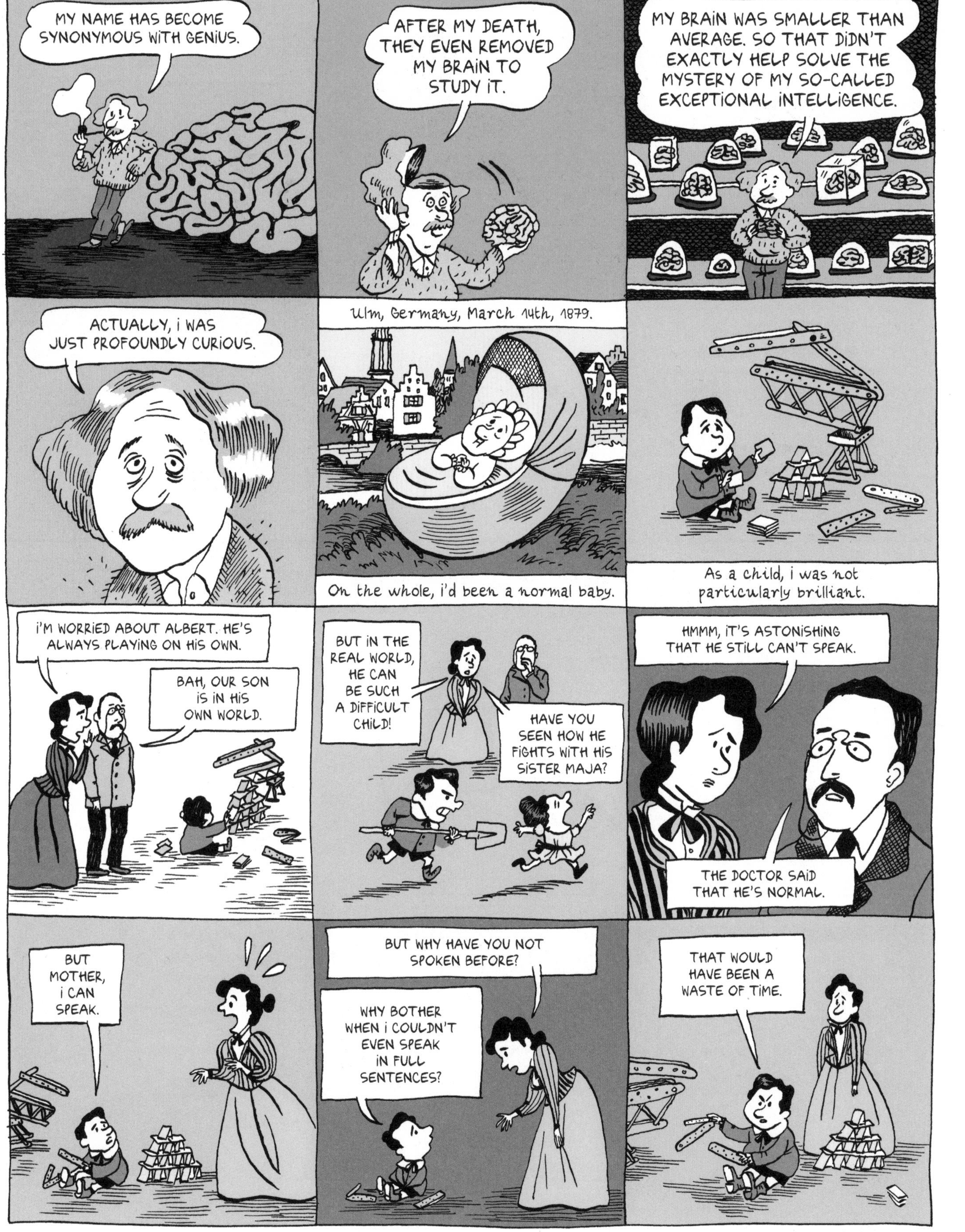

MY NAME HAS BECOME SYNONYMOUS WITH GENIUS.
AFTER MY DEATH, THEY EVEN REMOVED MY BRAIN TO STUDY IT.
MY BRAIN WAS SMALLER THAN AVERAGE. SO THAT DIDN'T EXACTLY HELP SOLVE THE MYSTERY OF MY SO-CALLED EXCEPTIONAL INTELLIGENCE.
ACTUALLY, I WAS JUST PROFOUNDLY CURIOUS.
Ulm, Germany, March 14th, 1879.
On the whole, I'd been a normal baby.
As a child, I was not particularly brilliant.
I'M WORRIED ABOUT ALBERT. HE'S ALWAYS PLAYING ON HIS OWN.
BAH, OUR SON IS IN HIS OWN WORLD.
BUT IN THE REAL WORLD, HE CAN BE SUCH A DIFFICULT CHILD!
HAVE YOU SEEN HOW HE FIGHTS WITH HIS SISTER MAJA?
HMMM, IT'S ASTONISHING THAT HE STILL CAN'T SPEAK.
THE DOCTOR SAID THAT HE'S NORMAL.
BUT MOTHER, I CAN SPEAK.
BUT WHY HAVE YOU NOT SPOKEN BEFORE?
WHY BOTHER WHEN I COULDN'T EVEN SPEAK IN FULL SENTENCES?
THAT WOULD HAVE BEEN A WASTE OF TIME.

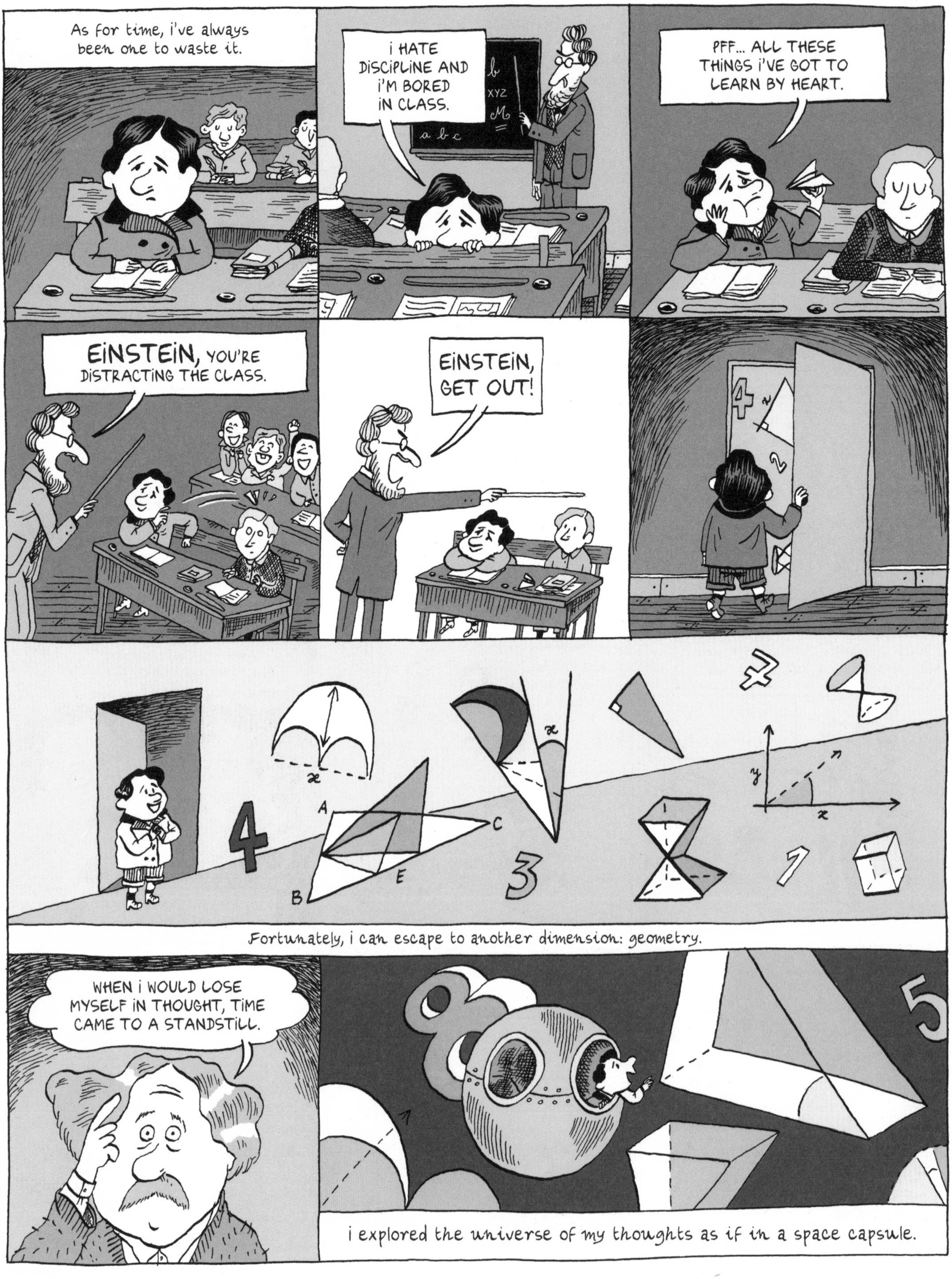

As for time, i've always been one to waste it.
i HATE DISCIPLINE AND i'M BORED iN CLASS.
PFF... ALL THESE THINGS i'VE GOT TO LEARN BY HEART.
EiNSTEiN, YOU'RE DiSTRACTING THE CLASS.
EiNSTEiN, GET OUT!
Fortunately, i can escape to another dimension: geometry.
WHEN i WOULD LOSE MYSELF iN THOUGHT, TiME CAME TO A STANDSTiLL.
i explored the universe of my thoughts as if in a space capsule.

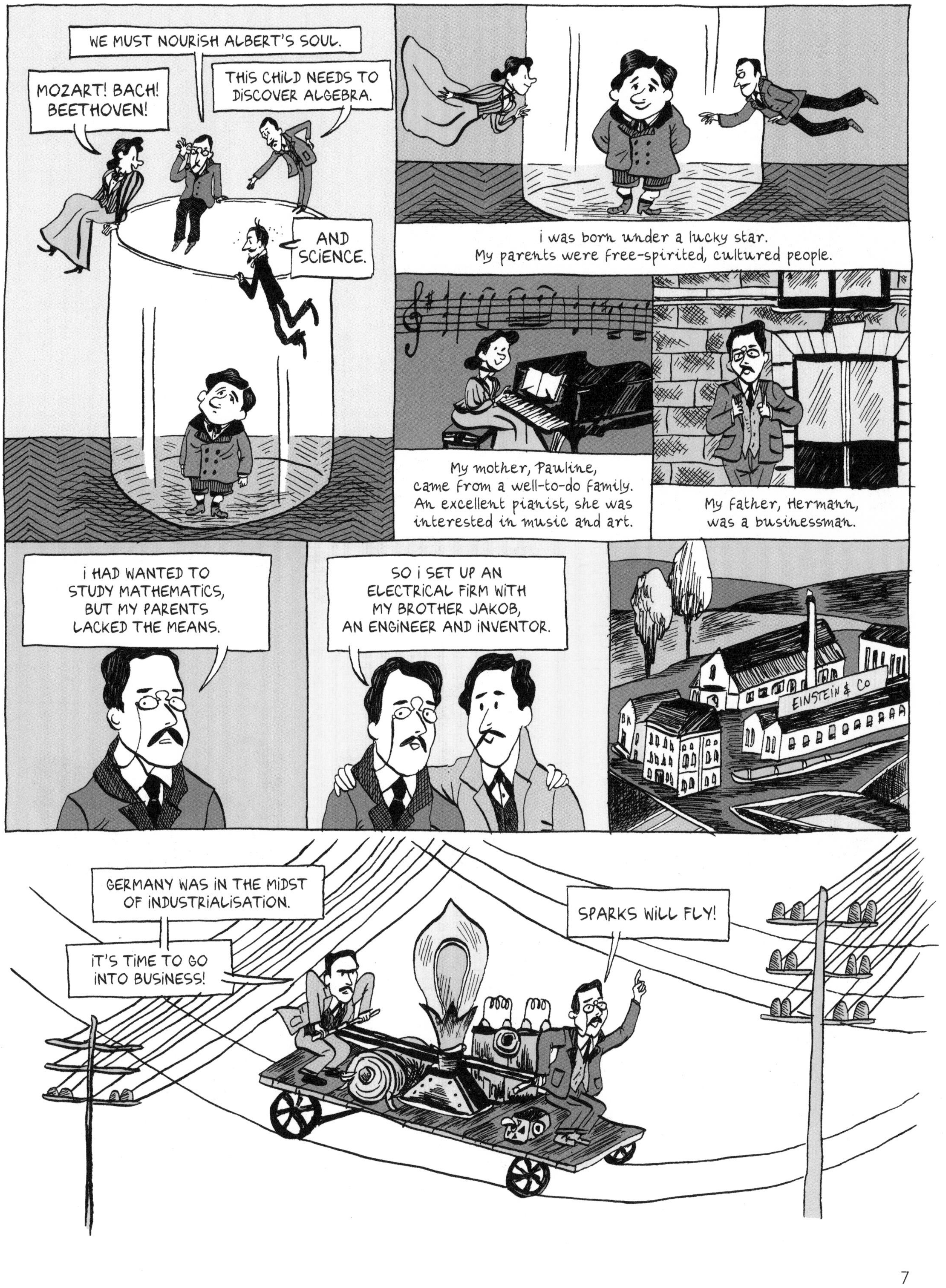
WE MUST NOURISH ALBERT'S SOUL.
MOZART! BACH! BEETHOVEN!
THIS CHILD NEEDS TO DISCOVER ALGEBRA.
AND SCIENCE.
I was born under a lucky star.
My parents were free-spirited, cultured people.
My mother, Pauline, came from a well-to-do family. An excellent pianist, she was interested in music and art.
My father, Hermann, was a businessman.
I HAD WANTED TO STUDY MATHEMATICS, BUT MY PARENTS LACKED THE MEANS.
SO I SET UP AN ELECTRICAL FIRM WITH MY BROTHER JAKOB, AN ENGINEER AND INVENTOR.
EINSTEIN & Co
GERMANY WAS IN THE MIDST OF INDUSTRIALISATION.
IT'S TIME TO GO INTO BUSINESS!
SPARKS WILL FLY!

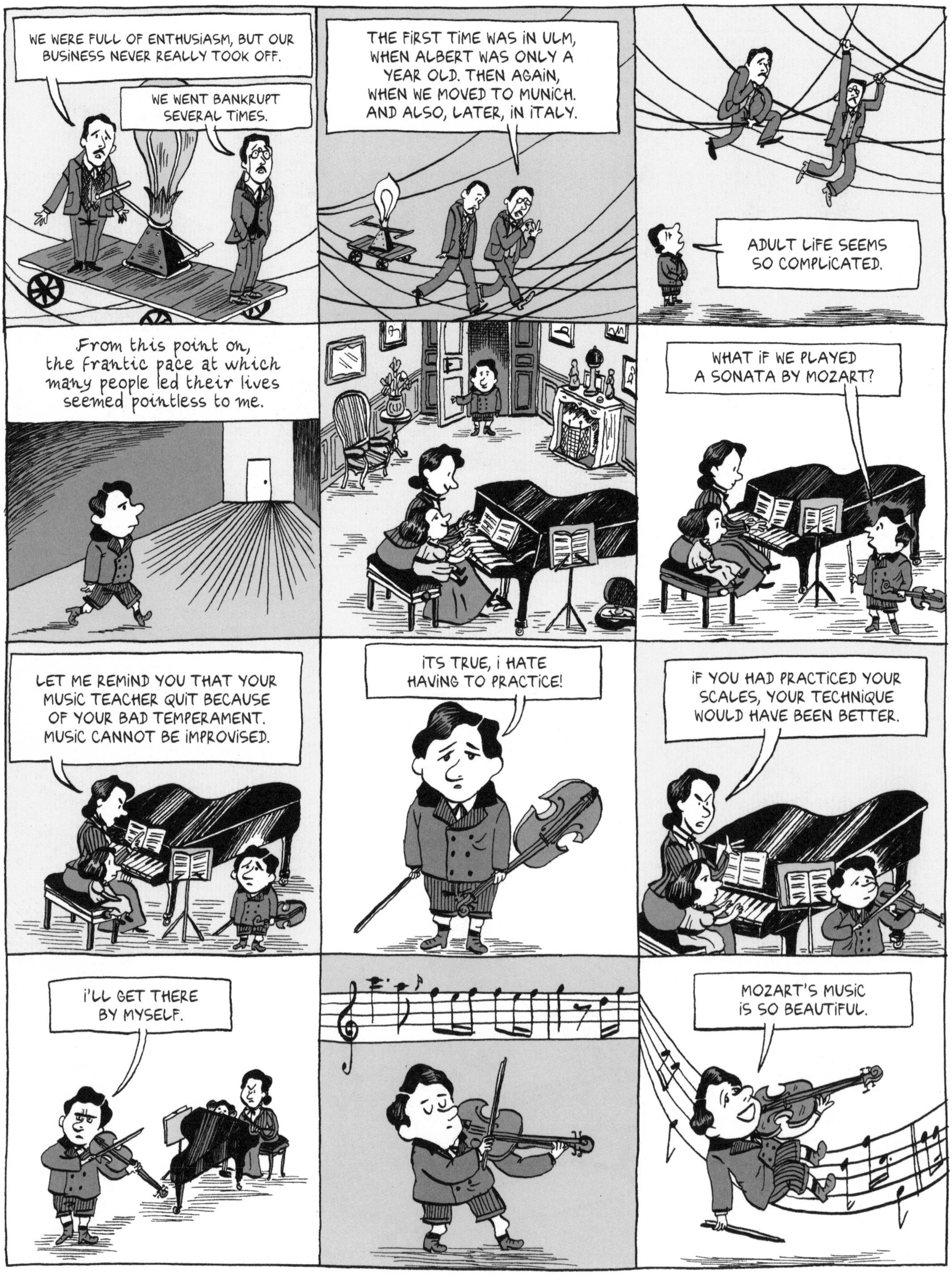
WE WERE FULL OF ENTHUSIASM, BUT OUR BUSINESS NEVER REALLY TOOK OFF.
WE WENT BANKRUPT SEVERAL TIMES.
THE FIRST TIME WAS IN ULM, WHEN ALBERT WAS ONLY A YEAR OLD. THEN AGAIN, WHEN WE MOVED TO MUNICH. AND ALSO, LATER, IN ITALY.
ADULT LIFE SEEMS SO COMPLICATED.
From this point on, the frantic pace at which many people led their lives seemed pointless to me.
WHAT IF WE PLAYED A SONATA BY MOZART?
LET ME REMIND YOU THAT YOUR MUSIC TEACHER QUIT BECAUSE OF YOUR BAD TEMPERAMENT. MUSIC CANNOT BE IMPROVISED.
ITS TRUE, I HATE HAVING TO PRACTICE!
IF YOU HAD PRACTICED YOUR SCALES, YOUR TECHNIQUE WOULD HAVE BEEN BETTER.
I'LL GET THERE BY MYSELF.
MOZART'S MUSIC IS SO BEAUTIFUL.

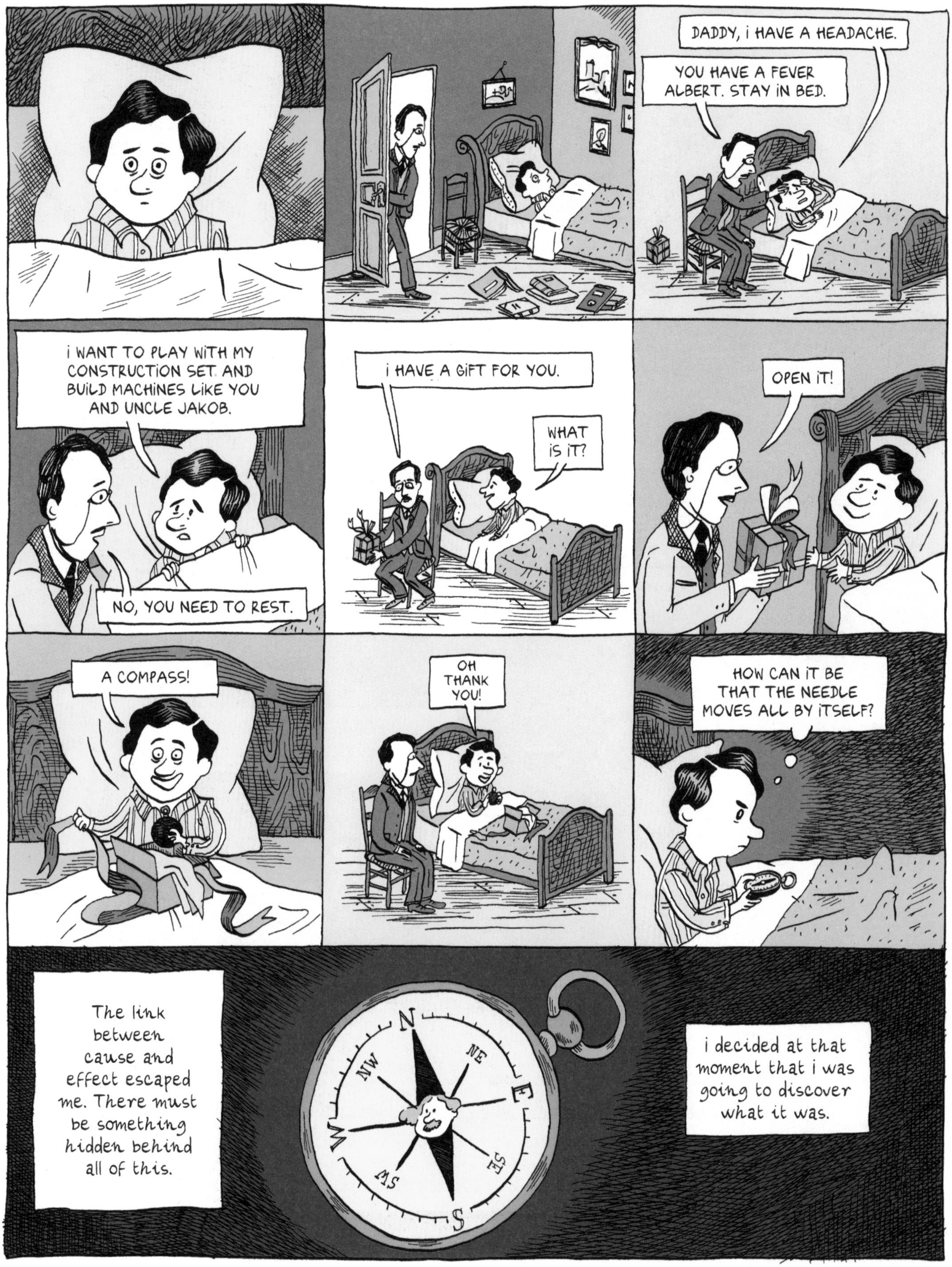
DADDY, i HAVE A HEADACHE.
YOU HAVE A FEVER ALBERT. STAY iN BED.
i WANT TO PLAY WiTH MY CONSTRUCTiON SET AND BUiLD MACHiNES LiKE YOU AND UNCLE JAKOB.
NO, YOU NEED TO REST.
i HAVE A GiFT FOR YOU.
WHAT iS iT?
OPEN iT!
A COMPASS!
OH THANK YOU!
HOW CAN iT BE THAT THE NEEDLE MOVES ALL BY iTSELF?
The link between cause and effect escaped me. There must be something hidden behind all of this.
N
NE
E
SE
S
SW
W
NW
i decided at that moment that i was going to discover what it was.

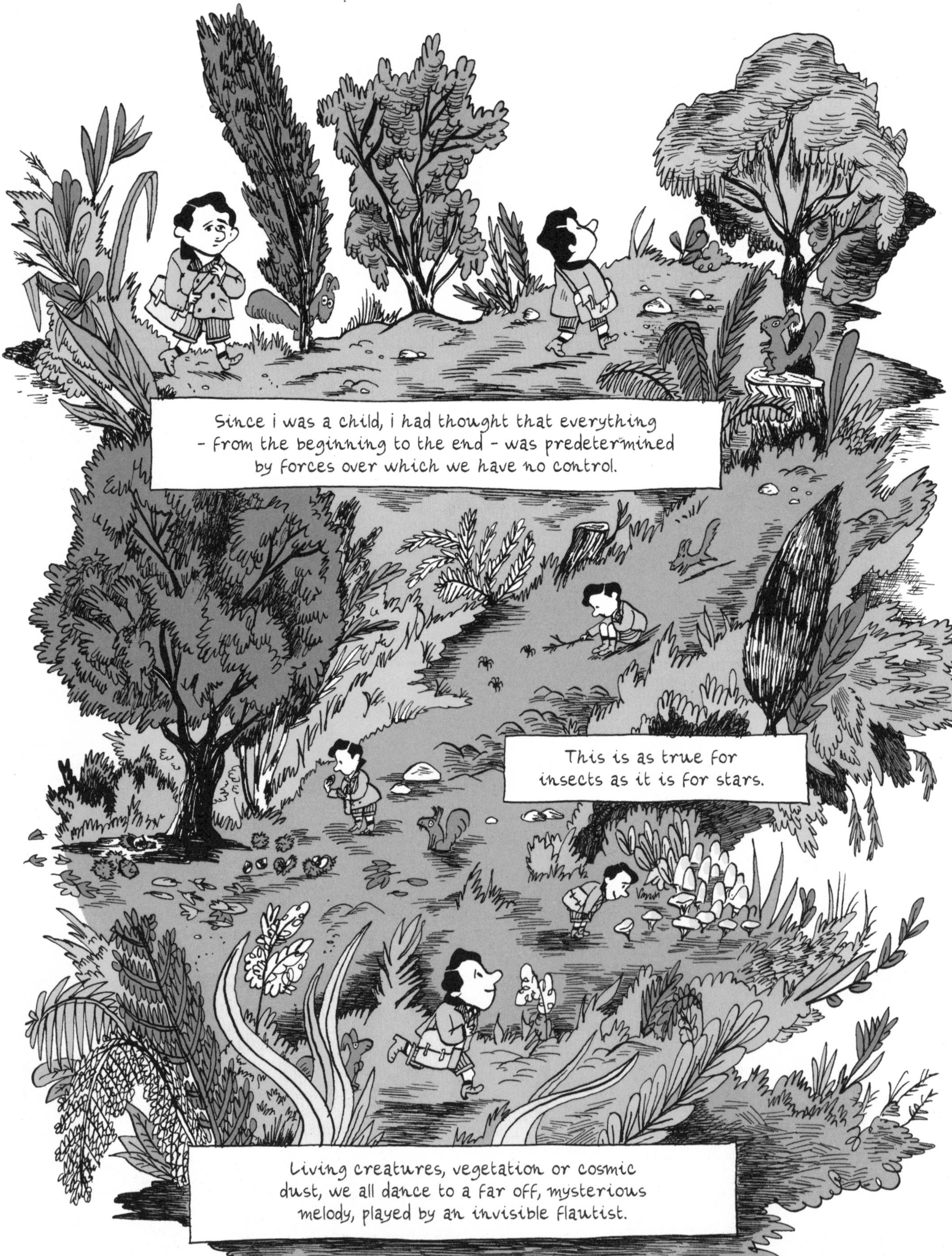
Since i was a child, i had thought that everything - from the beginning to the end - was predetermined by forces over which we have no control.
This is as true for insects as it is for stars.
Living creatures, vegetation or cosmic dust, we all dance to a far off, mysterious melody, played by an invisible flautist.

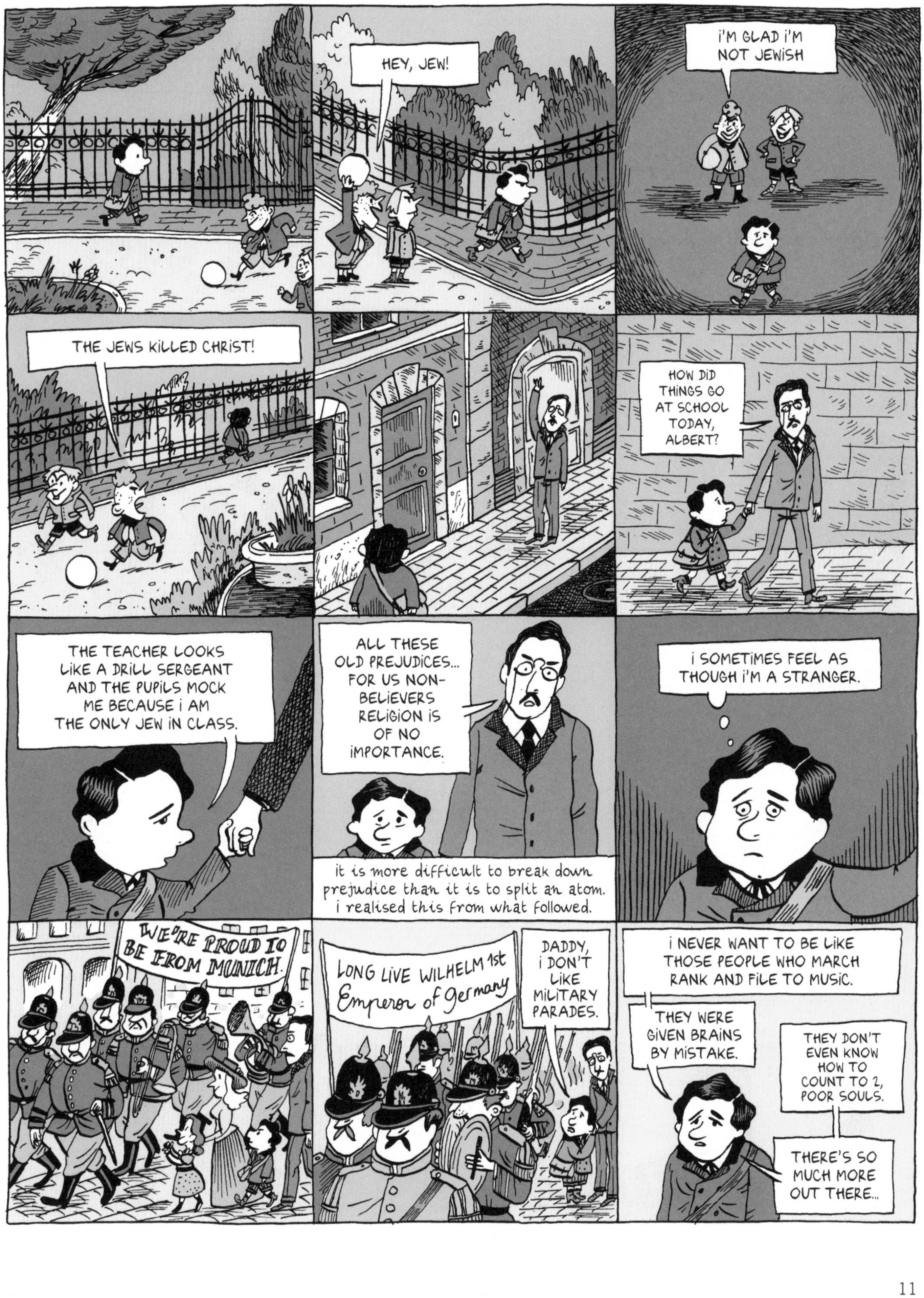
HEY, JEW!
I'M GLAD I'M NOT JEWISH
THE JEWS KILLED CHRIST!
HOW DID THINGS GO AT SCHOOL TODAY, ALBERT?
THE TEACHER LOOKS LIKE A DRILL SERGEANT AND THE PUPILS MOCK ME BECAUSE I AM THE ONLY JEW IN CLASS.
ALL THESE OLD PREJUDICES... FOR US NON-BELIEVERS RELIGION IS OF NO IMPORTANCE.
it is more difficult to break down prejudice than it is to split an atom. i realised this from what followed.
I SOMETIMES FEEL AS THOUGH I'M A STRANGER.
WE'RE PROUD TO BE FROM MUNICH
LONG LIVE WILHELM 1st Emperor of Germany
DADDY, I DON'T LIKE MILITARY PARADES.
I NEVER WANT TO BE LIKE THOSE PEOPLE WHO MARCH RANK AND FILE TO MUSIC.
THEY WERE GIVEN BRAINS BY MISTAKE.
THEY DON'T EVEN KNOW HOW TO COUNT TO 2, POOR SOULS.
THERE'S SO MUCH MORE OUT THERE...

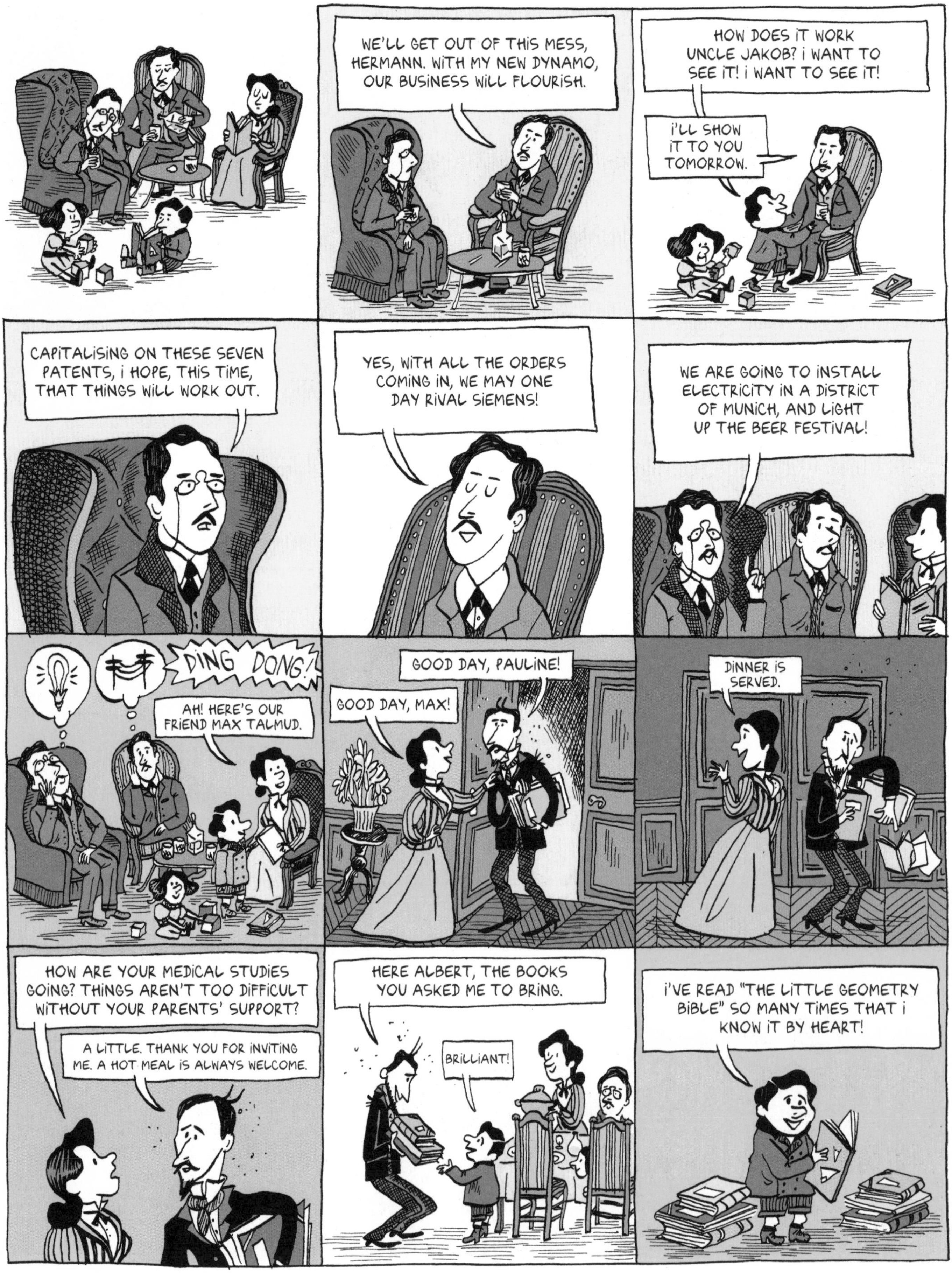
WE'LL GET OUT OF THIS MESS, HERMANN. WITH MY NEW DYNAMO, OUR BUSINESS WILL FLOURISH.
HOW DOES IT WORK UNCLE JAKOB? I WANT TO SEE IT! I WANT TO SEE IT!
I'LL SHOW IT TO YOU TOMORROW.
CAPITALISING ON THESE SEVEN PATENTS, I HOPE, THIS TIME, THAT THINGS WILL WORK OUT.
YES, WITH ALL THE ORDERS COMING IN, WE MAY ONE DAY RIVAL SIEMENS!
WE ARE GOING TO INSTALL ELECTRICITY IN A DISTRICT OF MUNICH, AND LIGHT UP THE BEER FESTIVAL!
DING DONG!
AH! HERE'S OUR FRIEND MAX TALMUD.
GOOD DAY, PAULINE!
GOOD DAY, MAX!
DINNER IS SERVED.
HOW ARE YOUR MEDICAL STUDIES GOING? THINGS AREN'T TOO DIFFICULT WITHOUT YOUR PARENTS' SUPPORT?
A LITTLE. THANK YOU FOR INVITING ME. A HOT MEAL IS ALWAYS WELCOME.
HERE ALBERT, THE BOOKS YOU ASKED ME TO BRING.
BRILLIANT!
I'VE READ "THE LITTLE GEOMETRY BIBLE" SO MANY TIMES THAT I KNOW IT BY HEART!

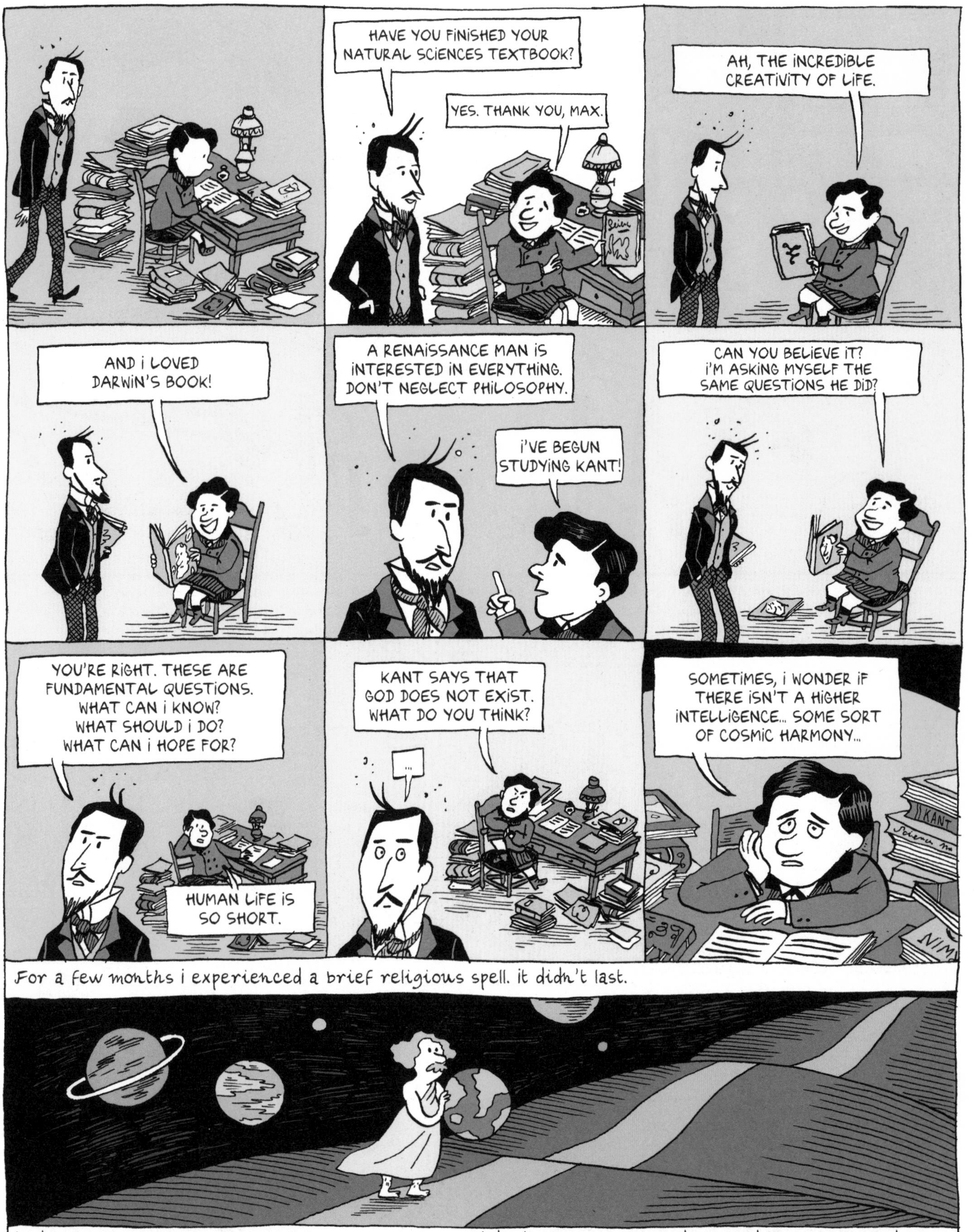
HAVE YOU FINISHED YOUR NATURAL SCIENCES TEXTBOOK?
YES. THANK YOU, MAX.
AH, THE INCREDIBLE CREATIVITY OF LIFE.
AND I LOVED DARWIN'S BOOK!
A RENAISSANCE MAN IS INTERESTED IN EVERYTHING. DON'T NEGLECT PHILOSOPHY.
I'VE BEGUN STUDYING KANT!
CAN YOU BELIEVE IT? I'M ASKING MYSELF THE SAME QUESTIONS HE DID?
YOU'RE RIGHT. THESE ARE FUNDAMENTAL QUESTIONS. WHAT CAN I KNOW? WHAT SHOULD I DO? WHAT CAN I HOPE FOR?
HUMAN LIFE IS SO SHORT.
KANT SAYS THAT GOD DOES NOT EXIST. WHAT DO YOU THINK?
...
SOMETIMES, I WONDER IF THERE ISN'T A HIGHER INTELLIGENCE... SOME SORT OF COSMIC HARMONY...
KANT
For a few months i experienced a brief religious spell. it didn't last.
i admire the structures of the universe, however i don't think that a God created them. He would have had to have an enormous brain. inconceivable!

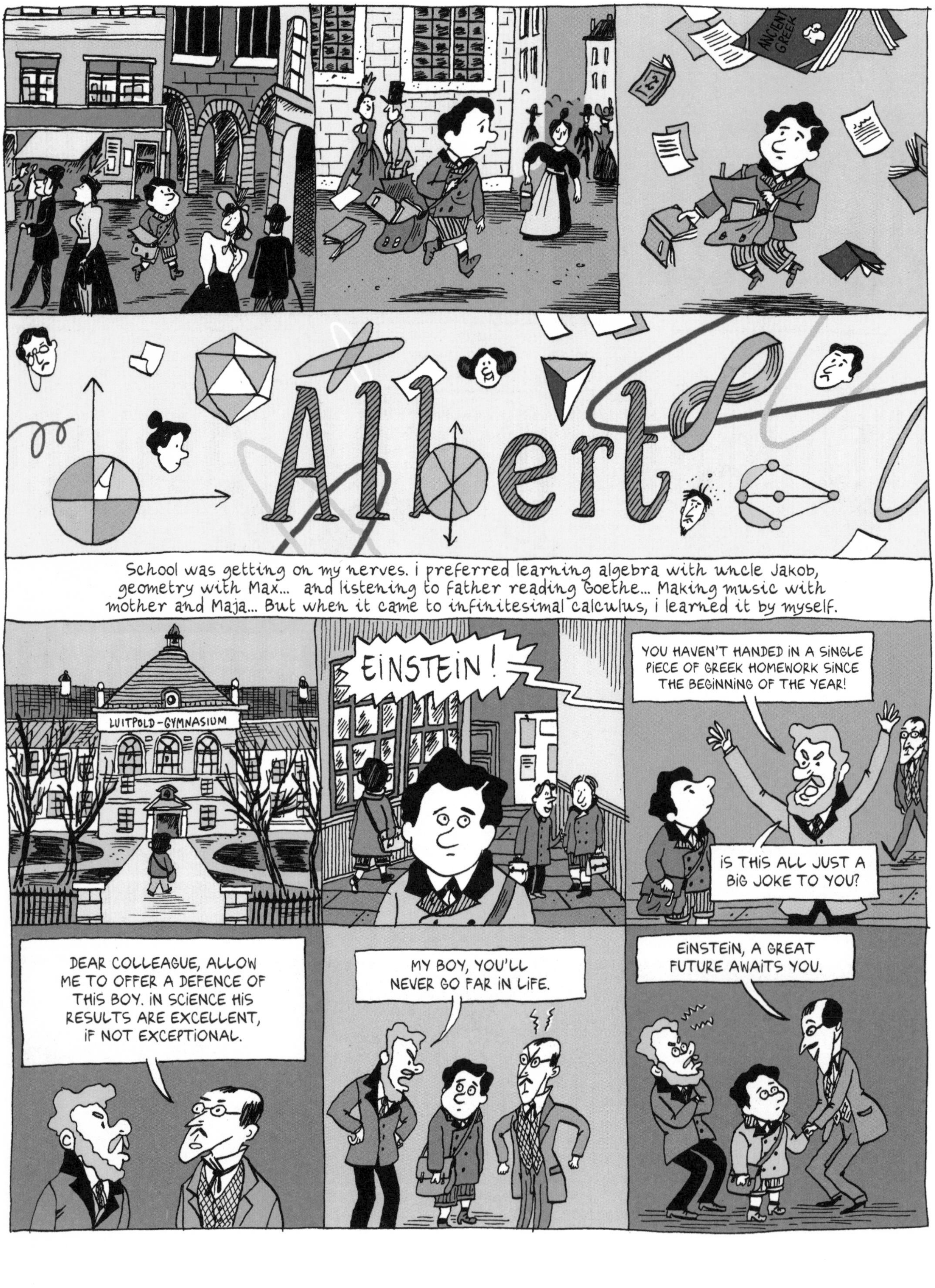

ANCIENT GREEK
Albert
School was getting on my nerves. i preferred learning algebra with uncle Jakob, geometry with Max... and listening to father reading Goethe... Making music with mother and Maja... But when it came to infinitesimal calculus, i learned it by myself.
LUITPOLD-GYMNASIUM
EINSTEIN!
YOU HAVEN'T HANDED IN A SINGLE PIECE OF GREEK HOMEWORK SINCE THE BEGINNING OF THE YEAR!
IS THIS ALL JUST A BIG JOKE TO YOU?
DEAR COLLEAGUE, ALLOW ME TO OFFER A DEFENCE OF THIS BOY. IN SCIENCE HIS RESULTS ARE EXCELLENT, IF NOT EXCEPTIONAL.
MY BOY, YOU'LL NEVER GO FAR IN LIFE.
EINSTEIN, A GREAT FUTURE AWAITS YOU.

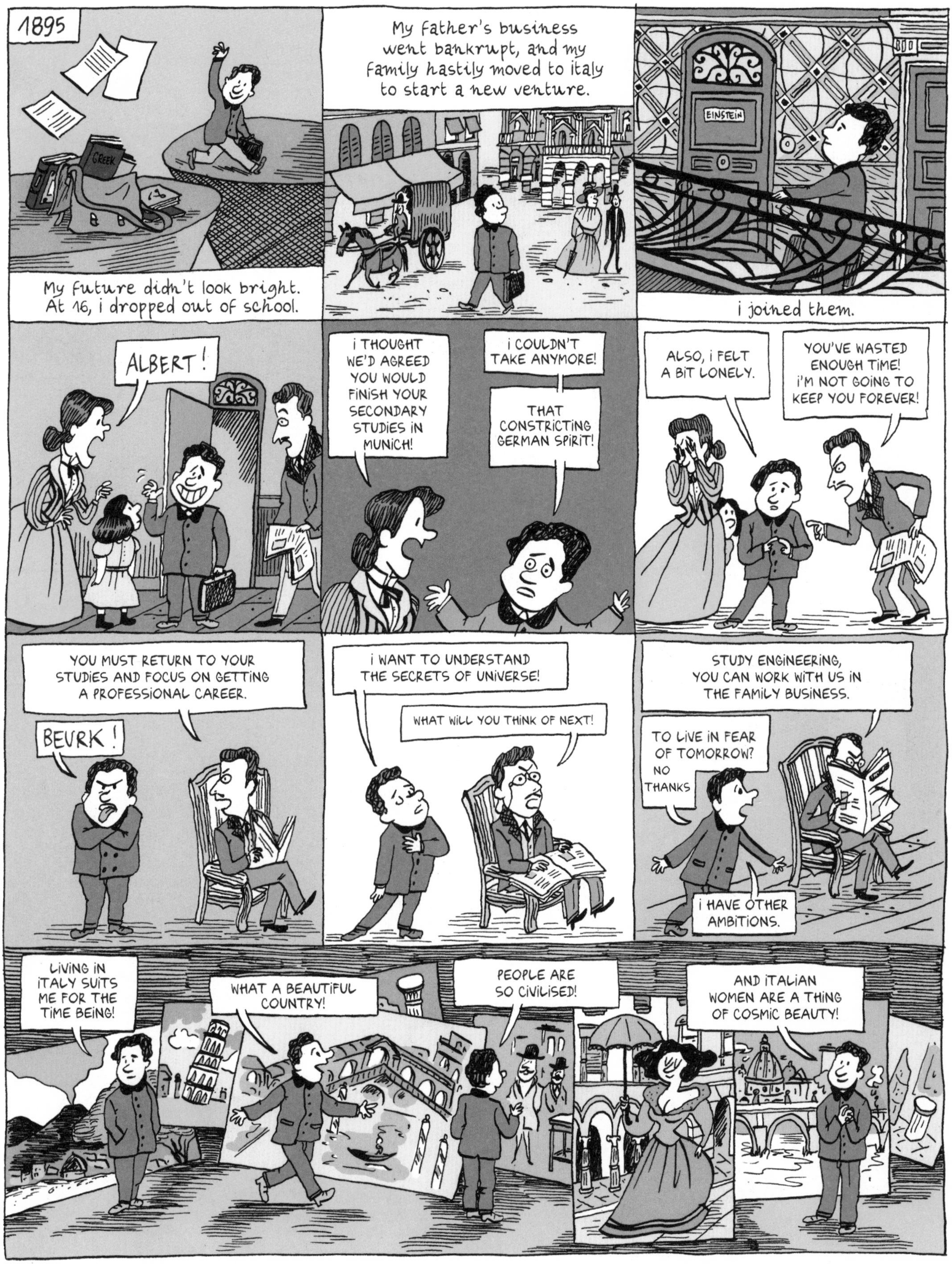
1895
GREEK
My future didn't look bright. At 16, i dropped out of school.
My father's business went bankrupt, and my family hastily moved to italy to start a new venture.
EINSTEIN
i joined them.
ALBERT!
i THOUGHT WE'D AGREED YOU WOULD FiNiSH YOUR SECONDARY STUDiES iN MUNiCH!
i COULDN'T TAKE ANYMORE!
THAT CONSTRiCTiNG GERMAN SPiRiT!
ALSO, i FELT A BiT LONELY.
YOU'VE WASTED ENOUGH TiME! i'M NOT GOING TO KEEP YOU FOREVER!
YOU MUST RETURN TO YOUR STUDiES AND FOCUS ON GETTiNG A PROFESSiONAL CAREER.
BEURK!
i WANT TO UNDERSTAND THE SECRETS OF UNiVERSE!
WHAT WiLL YOU THiNK OF NEXT!
STUDY ENGiNEERiNG, YOU CAN WORK WiTH US iN THE FAMiLY BUSiNESS.
TO LiVE iN FEAR OF TOMORROW?
NO THANKS
i HAVE OTHER AMBiTiONS.
LiViNG iN iTALY SUiTS ME FOR THE TiME BEiNG!
WHAT A BEAUTiFUL COUNTRY!
PEOPLE ARE SO CiViLiSED!
AND iTALiAN WOMEN ARE A THiNG OF COSMiC BEAUTY!

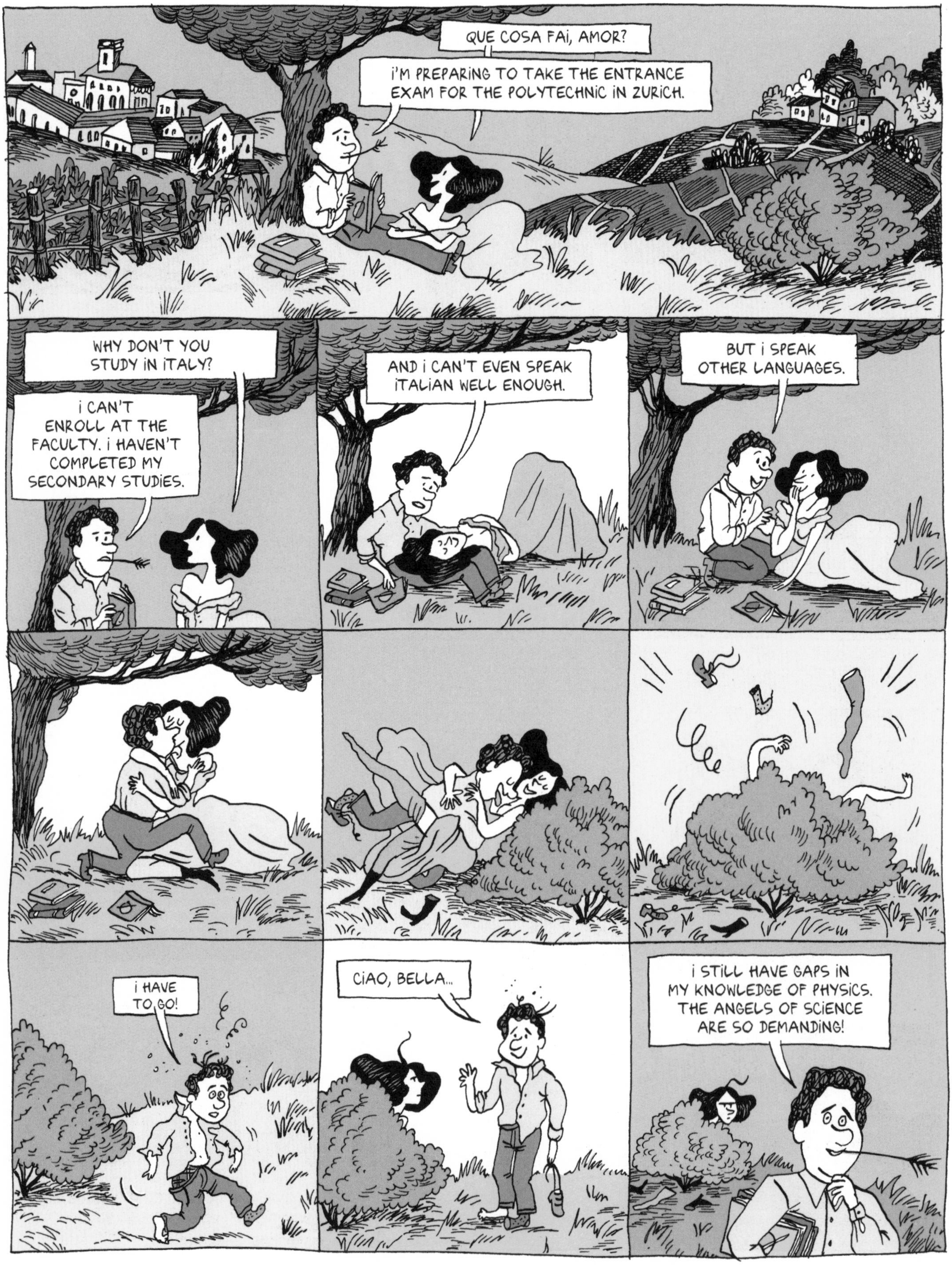
QUE COSA FAi, AMOR?
i'M PREPARiNG TO TAKE THE ENTRANCE EXAM FOR THE POLYTECHNiC iN ZURiCH.
WHY DON'T YOU STUDY iN iTALY?
i CAN'T ENROLL AT THE FACULTY. i HAVEN'T COMPLETED MY SECONDARY STUDiES.
AND i CAN'T EVEN SPEAK iTALiAN WELL ENOUGH.
BUT i SPEAK OTHER LANGUAGES.
i HAVE TO GO!
CiAO, BELLA...
i STiLL HAVE GAPS iN MY KNOWLEDGE OF PHYSiCS. THE ANGELS OF SCiENCE ARE SO DEMANDiNG!

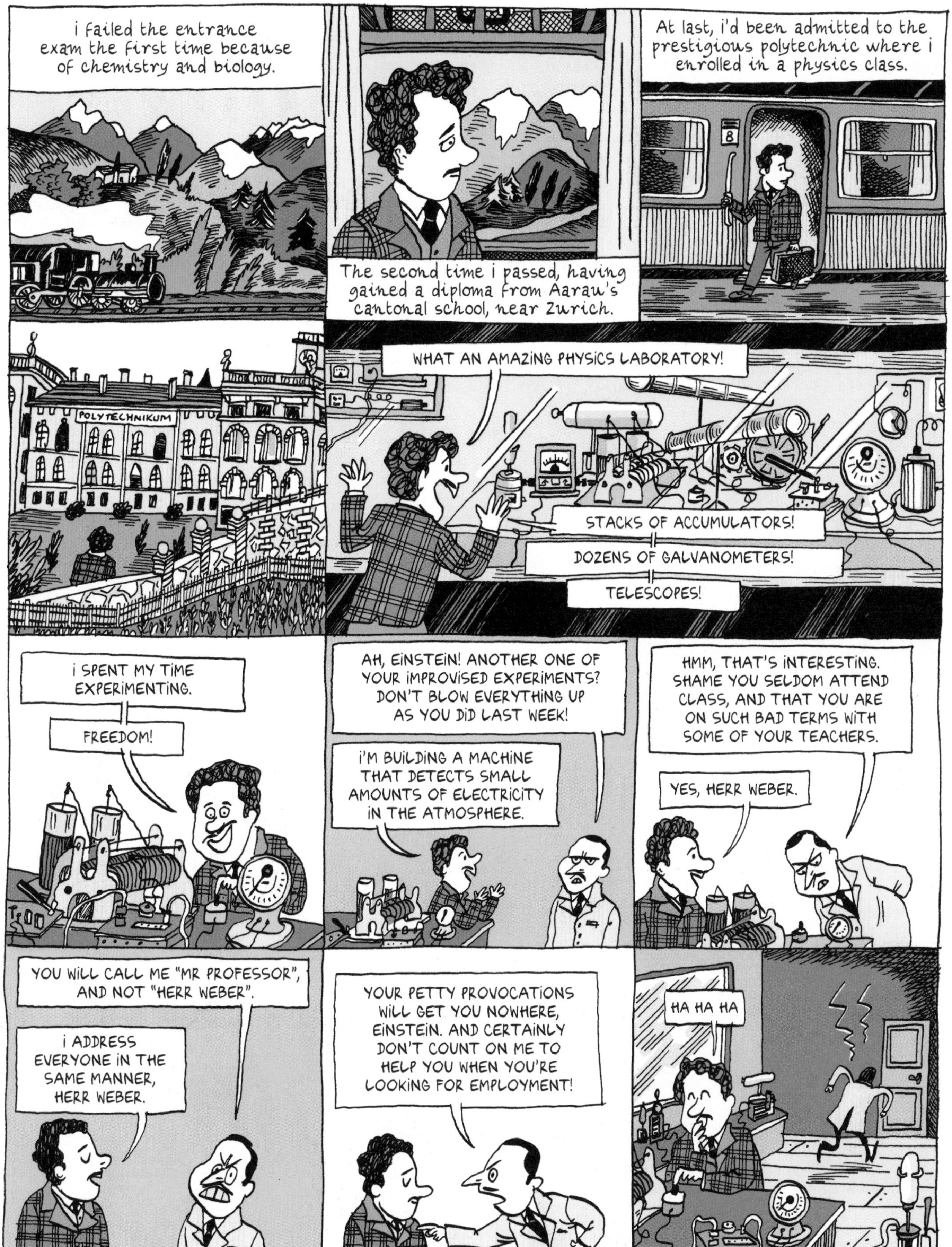
i failed the entrance exam the first time because of chemistry and biology.
The second time i passed, having gained a diploma from Aarau's cantonal school, near Zurich.
At last, i'd been admitted to the prestigious polytechnic where i enrolled in a physics class.
POLYTECHNIKUM
WHAT AN AMAZING PHYSICS LABORATORY!
STACKS OF ACCUMULATORS!
DOZENS OF GALVANOMETERS!
TELESCOPES!
i SPENT MY TiME EXPERiMENTiNG.
FREEDOM!
AH, EiNSTEiN! ANOTHER ONE OF YOUR iMPROViSED EXPERiMENTS? DON'T BLOW EVERYTHiNG UP AS YOU DiD LAST WEEK!
i'M BUiLDiNG A MACHiNE THAT DETECTS SMALL AMOUNTS OF ELECTRiCiTY iN THE ATMOSPHERE.
HMM, THAT'S iNTERESTiNG. SHAME YOU SELDOM ATTEND CLASS, AND THAT YOU ARE ON SUCH BAD TERMS WiTH SOME OF YOUR TEACHERS.
YES, HERR WEBER.
YOU WiLL CALL ME "MR PROFESSOR", AND NOT "HERR WEBER".
i ADDRESS EVERYONE iN THE SAME MANNER, HERR WEBER.
YOUR PETTY PROVOCATiONS WiLL GET YOU NOWHERE, EiNSTEiN. AND CERTAiNLY DON'T COUNT ON ME TO HELP YOU WHEN YOU'RE LOOKiNG FOR EMPLOYMENT!
HA HA HA

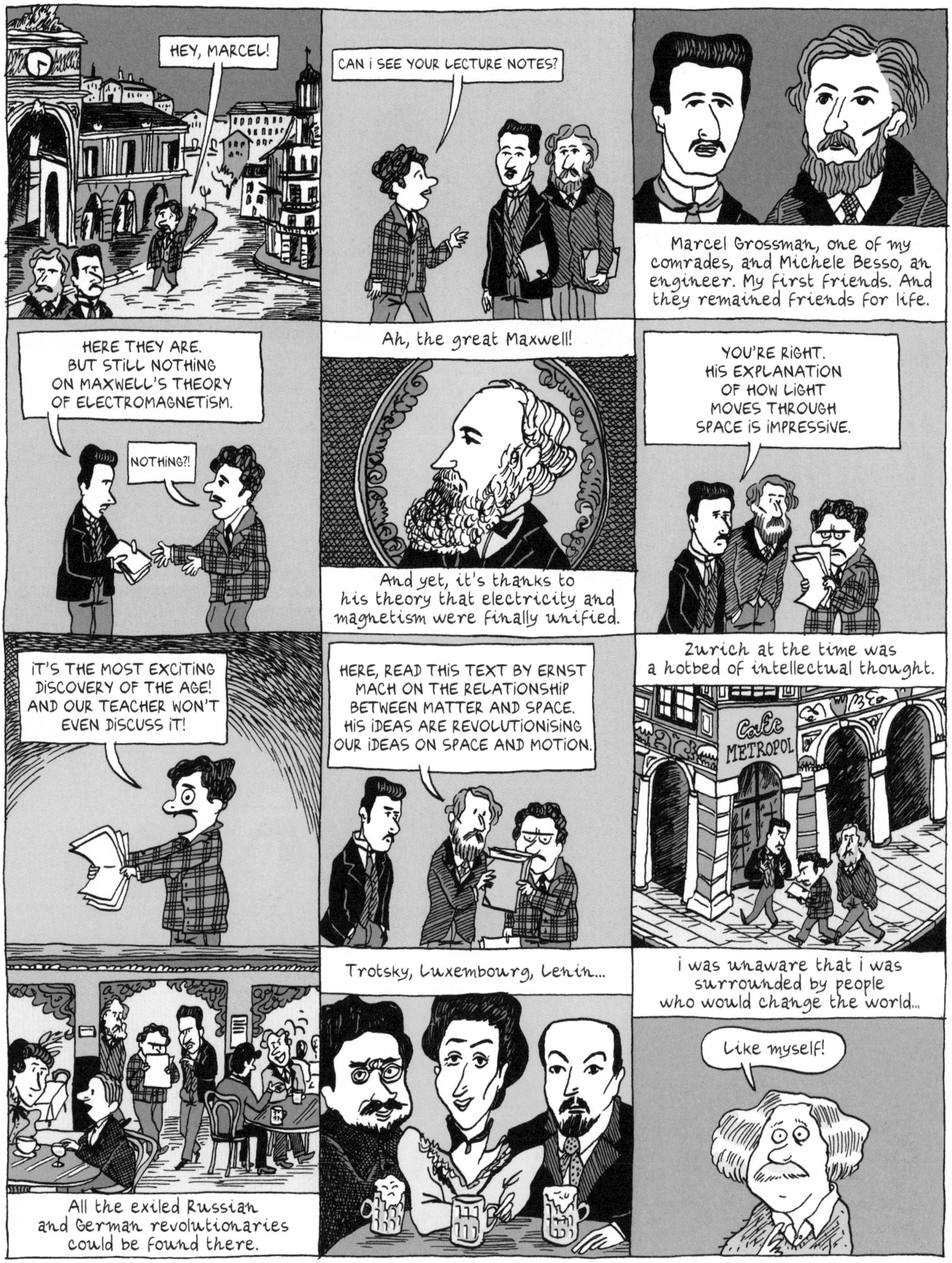
HEY, MARCEL!
CAN I SEE YOUR LECTURE NOTES?
Ah, the great Maxwell!
Marcel Grossman, one of my comrades, and Michele Besso, an engineer. My first friends. And they remained friends for life.
HERE THEY ARE. BUT STILL NOTHING ON MAXWELL'S THEORY OF ELECTROMAGNETISM.
NOTHING?!
And yet, it's thanks to his theory that electricity and magnetism were finally unified.
YOU'RE RIGHT. HIS EXPLANATION OF HOW LIGHT MOVES THROUGH SPACE IS IMPRESSIVE.
IT'S THE MOST EXCITING DISCOVERY OF THE AGE! AND OUR TEACHER WON'T EVEN DISCUSS IT!
HERE, READ THIS TEXT BY ERNST MACH ON THE RELATIONSHIP BETWEEN MATTER AND SPACE. HIS IDEAS ARE REVOLUTIONISING OUR IDEAS ON SPACE AND MOTION.
Zurich at the time was a hotbed of intellectual thought.
Café METROPOL
All the exiled Russian and German revolutionaries could be found there.
Trotsky, Luxembourg, Lenin...
I was unaware that I was surrounded by people who would change the world...
Like myself!

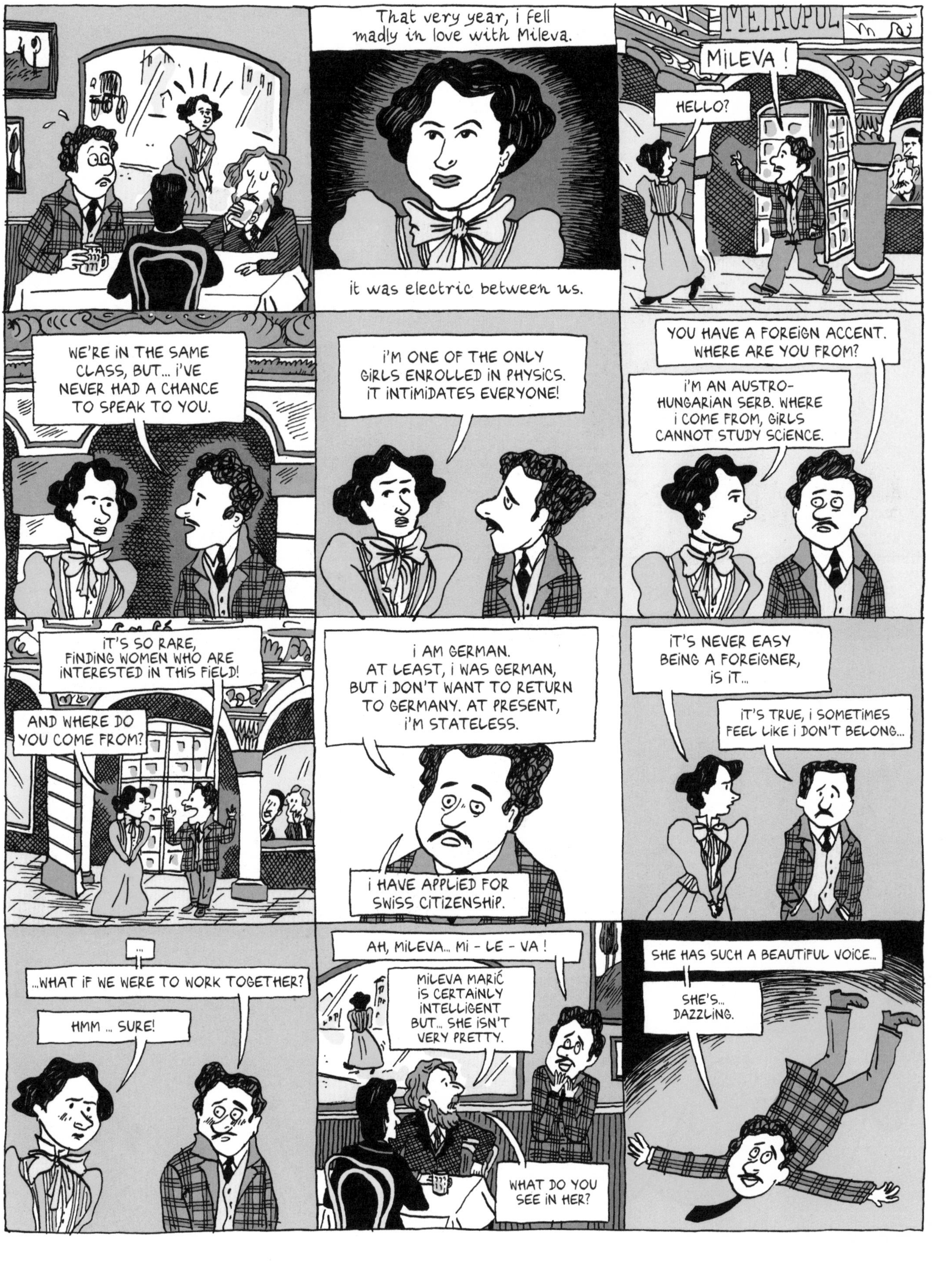

That very year, i fell madly in love with Mileva.
it was electric between us.
MiLEVA !
HELLO?
WE'RE iN THE SAME CLASS, BUT... i'VE NEVER HAD A CHANCE TO SPEAK TO YOU.
i'M ONE OF THE ONLY GiRLS ENROLLED iN PHYSiCS. iT iNTiMiDATES EVERYONE!
YOU HAVE A FOREiGN ACCENT. WHERE ARE YOU FROM?
i'M AN AUSTRO-HUNGARiAN SERB. WHERE i COME FROM, GiRLS CANNOT STUDY SCiENCE.
iT'S SO RARE, FiNDiNG WOMEN WHO ARE iNTERESTED iN THiS FiELD!
AND WHERE DO YOU COME FROM?
i AM GERMAN. AT LEAST, i WAS GERMAN, BUT i DON'T WANT TO RETURN TO GERMANY. AT PRESENT, i'M STATELESS.
i HAVE APPLiED FOR SWiSS CiTiZENSHiP.
iT'S NEVER EASY BEiNG A FOREiGNER, iS iT...
iT'S TRUE, i SOMETiMES FEEL LiKE i DON'T BELONG...
...
...WHAT iF WE WERE TO WORK TOGETHER?
HMM ... SURE!
AH, MiLEVA... Mi - LE - VA !
MiLEVA MARiĆ iS CERTAiNLY iNTELLiGENT BUT... SHE iSN'T VERY PRETTY.
WHAT DO YOU SEE iN HER?
SHE HAS SUCH A BEAUTiFUL VOiCE...
SHE'S... DAZZLiNG.

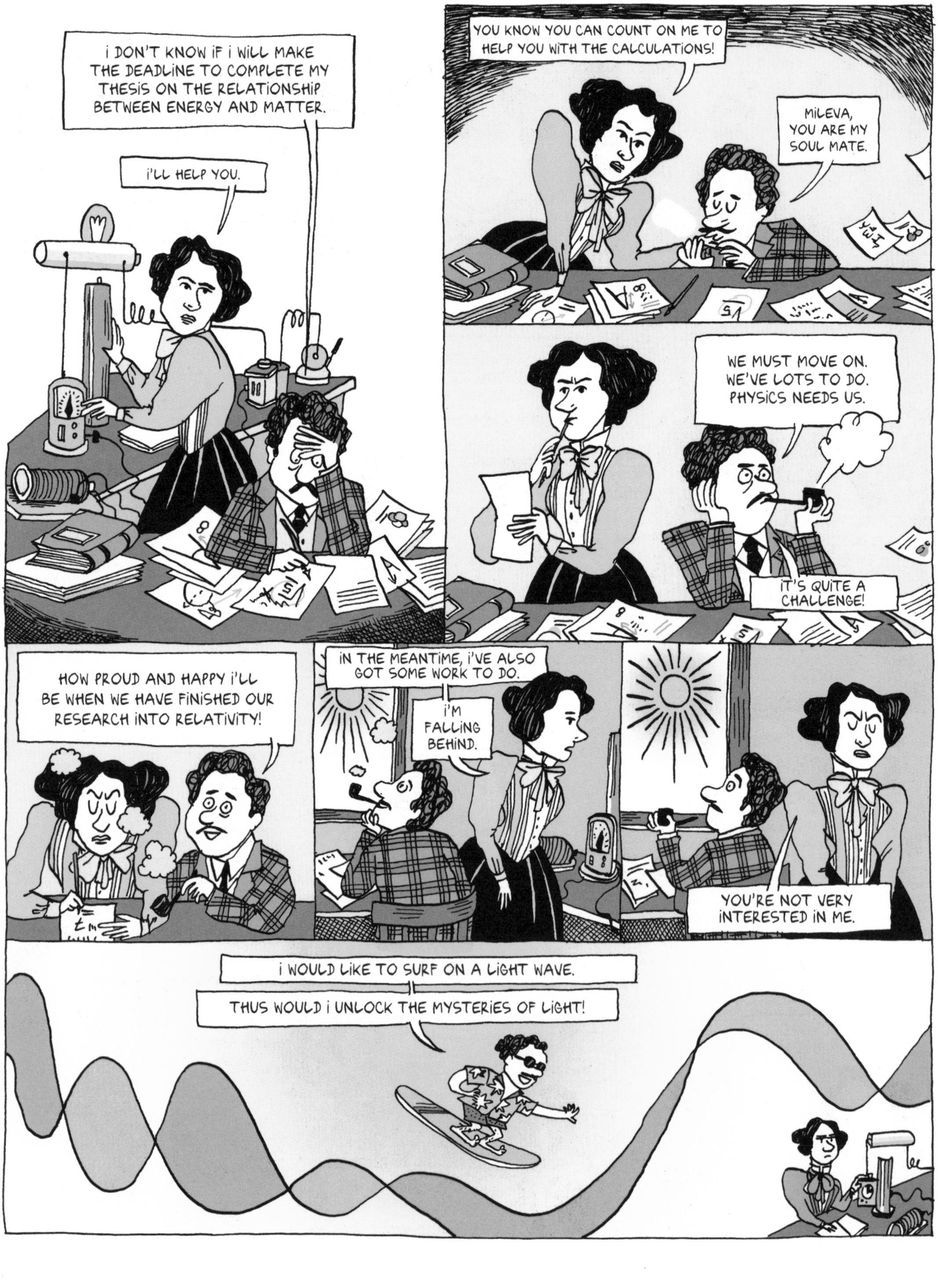
I DON'T KNOW IF I WILL MAKE THE DEADLINE TO COMPLETE MY THESIS ON THE RELATIONSHIP BETWEEN ENERGY AND MATTER.
I'LL HELP YOU.
YOU KNOW YOU CAN COUNT ON ME TO HELP YOU WITH THE CALCULATIONS!
MILEVA, YOU ARE MY SOUL MATE.
WE MUST MOVE ON. WE'VE LOTS TO DO. PHYSICS NEEDS US.
IT'S QUITE A CHALLENGE!
HOW PROUD AND HAPPY I'LL BE WHEN WE HAVE FINISHED OUR RESEARCH INTO RELATIVITY!
IN THE MEANTIME, I'VE ALSO GOT SOME WORK TO DO.
I'M FALLING BEHIND.
YOU'RE NOT VERY INTERESTED IN ME.
I WOULD LIKE TO SURF ON A LIGHT WAVE.
THUS WOULD I UNLOCK THE MYSTERIES OF LIGHT!

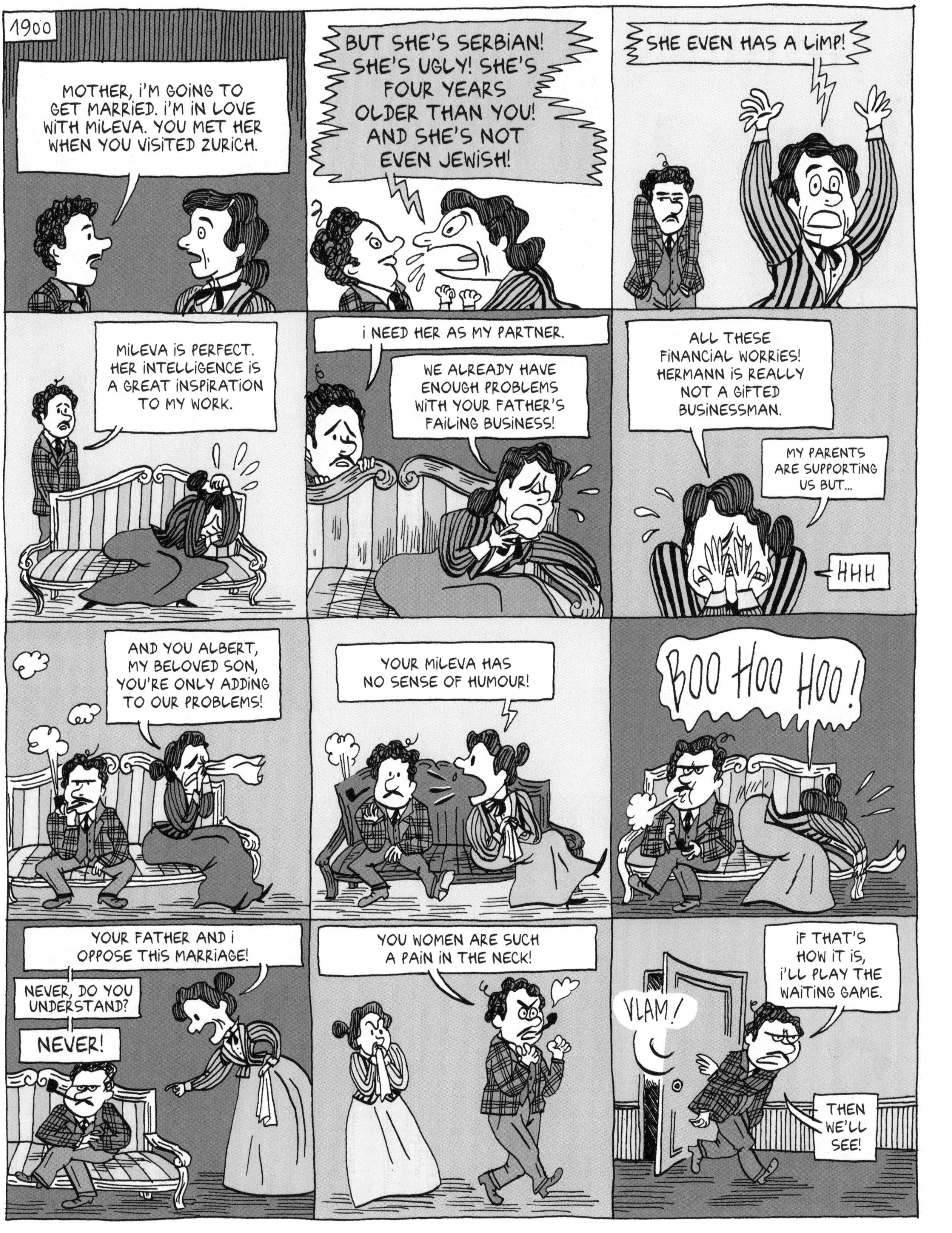
1900
MOTHER, I'M GOING TO GET MARRIED. I'M IN LOVE WITH MILEVA. YOU MET HER WHEN YOU VISITED ZURICH.
BUT SHE'S SERBIAN! SHE'S UGLY! SHE'S FOUR YEARS OLDER THAN YOU! AND SHE'S NOT EVEN JEWISH!
SHE EVEN HAS A LIMP!
MILEVA IS PERFECT. HER INTELLIGENCE IS A GREAT INSPIRATION TO MY WORK.
I NEED HER AS MY PARTNER.
WE ALREADY HAVE ENOUGH PROBLEMS WITH YOUR FATHER'S FAILING BUSINESS!
ALL THESE FINANCIAL WORRIES! HERMANN IS REALLY NOT A GIFTED BUSINESSMAN.
MY PARENTS ARE SUPPORTING US BUT...
HHH
AND YOU ALBERT, MY BELOVED SON, YOU'RE ONLY ADDING TO OUR PROBLEMS!
YOUR MILEVA HAS NO SENSE OF HUMOUR!
BOO HOO HOO!
YOUR FATHER AND I OPPOSE THIS MARRIAGE!
NEVER, DO YOU UNDERSTAND?
NEVER!
YOU WOMEN ARE SUCH A PAIN IN THE NECK!
IF THAT'S HOW IT IS, I'LL PLAY THE WAITING GAME.
VLAM!
THEN WE'LL SEE!

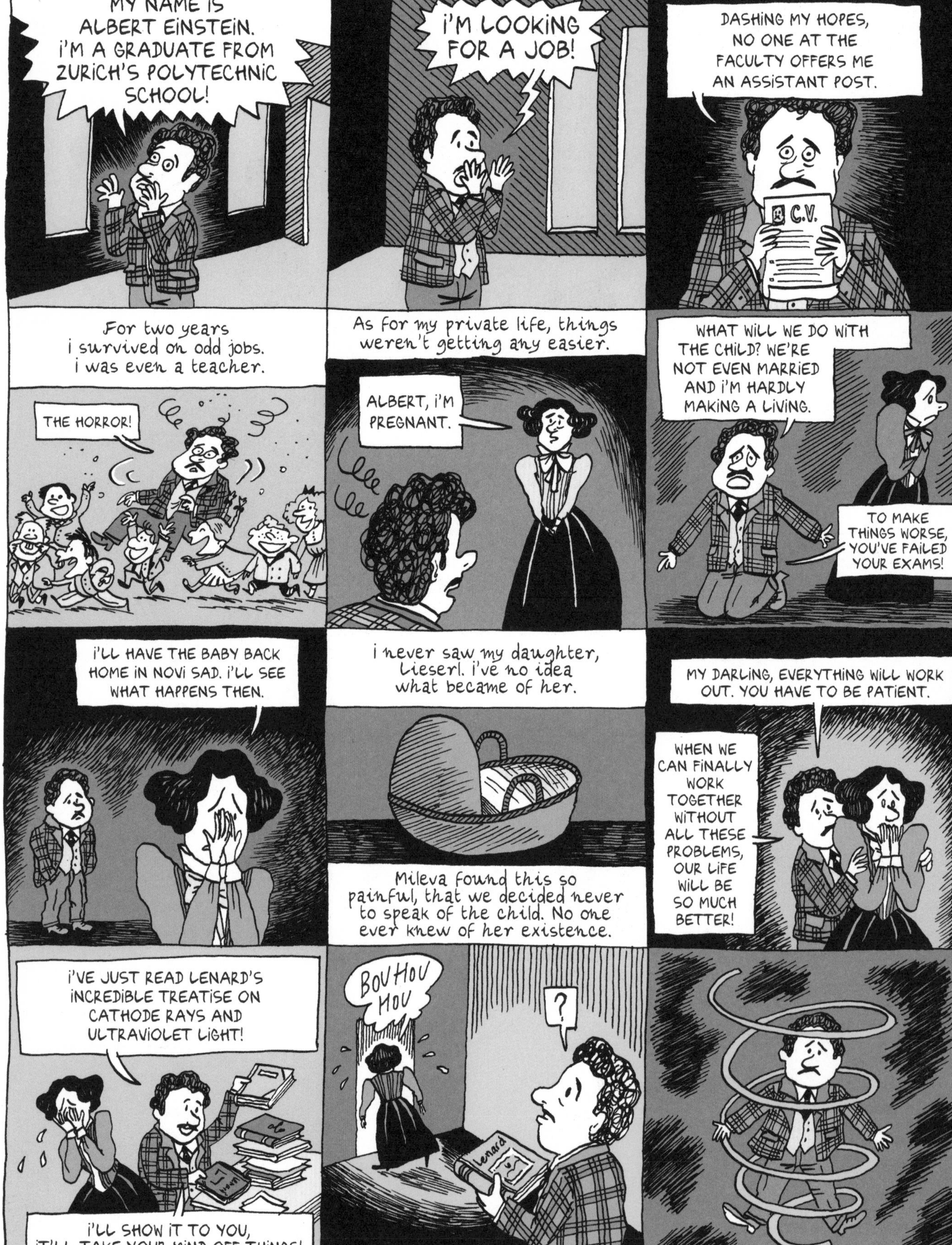
MY NAME IS ALBERT EINSTEIN. I'M A GRADUATE FROM ZURICH'S POLYTECHNIC SCHOOL!
I'M LOOKING FOR A JOB!
DASHING MY HOPES, NO ONE AT THE FACULTY OFFERS ME AN ASSISTANT POST.
C.V.
For two years I survived on odd jobs. I was even a teacher.
THE HORROR!
As for my private life, things weren't getting any easier.
ALBERT, I'M PREGNANT.
WHAT WILL WE DO WITH THE CHILD? WE'RE NOT EVEN MARRIED AND I'M HARDLY MAKING A LIVING.
TO MAKE THINGS WORSE, YOU'VE FAILED YOUR EXAMS!
I'LL HAVE THE BABY BACK HOME IN NOVI SAD. I'LL SEE WHAT HAPPENS THEN.
I never saw my daughter, Lieserl. I've no idea what became of her.
Mileva found this so painful, that we decided never to speak of the child. No one ever knew of her existence.
MY DARLING, EVERYTHING WILL WORK OUT. YOU HAVE TO BE PATIENT.
WHEN WE CAN FINALLY WORK TOGETHER WITHOUT ALL THESE PROBLEMS, OUR LIFE WILL BE SO MUCH BETTER!
I'VE JUST READ LENARD'S INCREDIBLE TREATISE ON CATHODE RAYS AND ULTRAVIOLET LIGHT!
I'LL SHOW IT TO YOU, IT'LL TAKE YOUR MIND OFF THINGS!
BOU HOU HOU
?
Lenard

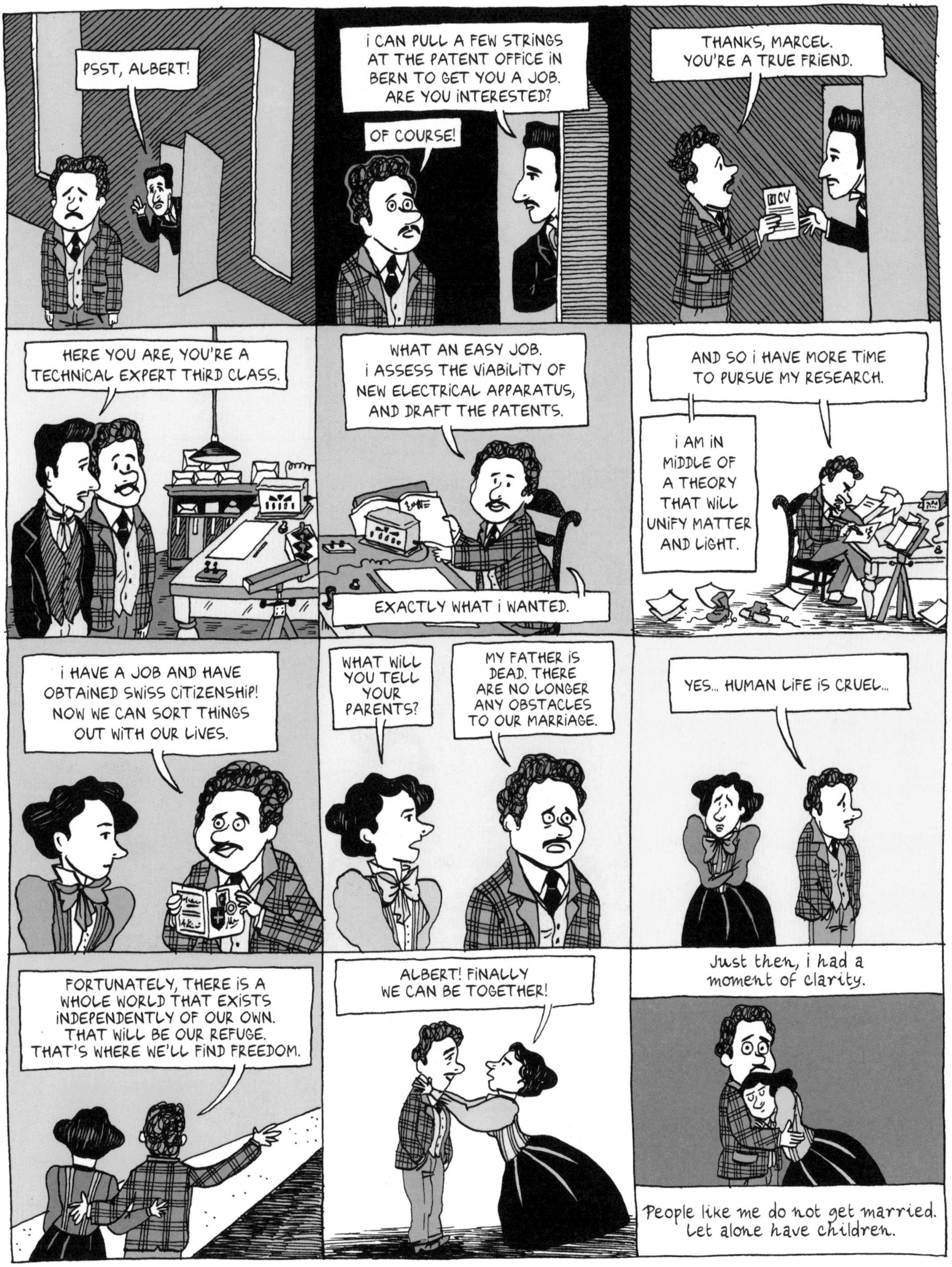
PSST, ALBERT!
I CAN PULL A FEW STRINGS AT THE PATENT OFFICE IN BERN TO GET YOU A JOB. ARE YOU INTERESTED?
OF COURSE!
THANKS, MARCEL. YOU'RE A TRUE FRIEND.
CV
HERE YOU ARE, YOU'RE A TECHNICAL EXPERT THIRD CLASS.
WHAT AN EASY JOB. I ASSESS THE VIABILITY OF NEW ELECTRICAL APPARATUS, AND DRAFT THE PATENTS.
EXACTLY WHAT I WANTED.
AND SO I HAVE MORE TIME TO PURSUE MY RESEARCH.
I AM IN MIDDLE OF A THEORY THAT WILL UNIFY MATTER AND LIGHT.
I HAVE A JOB AND HAVE OBTAINED SWISS CITIZENSHIP! NOW WE CAN SORT THINGS OUT WITH OUR LIVES.
WHAT WILL YOU TELL YOUR PARENTS?
MY FATHER IS DEAD. THERE ARE NO LONGER ANY OBSTACLES TO OUR MARRIAGE.
YES... HUMAN LIFE IS CRUEL...
FORTUNATELY, THERE IS A WHOLE WORLD THAT EXISTS INDEPENDENTLY OF OUR OWN. THAT WILL BE OUR REFUGE. THAT'S WHERE WE'LL FIND FREEDOM.
ALBERT! FINALLY WE CAN BE TOGETHER!
Just then, I had a moment of clarity.
People like me do not get married. Let alone have children.

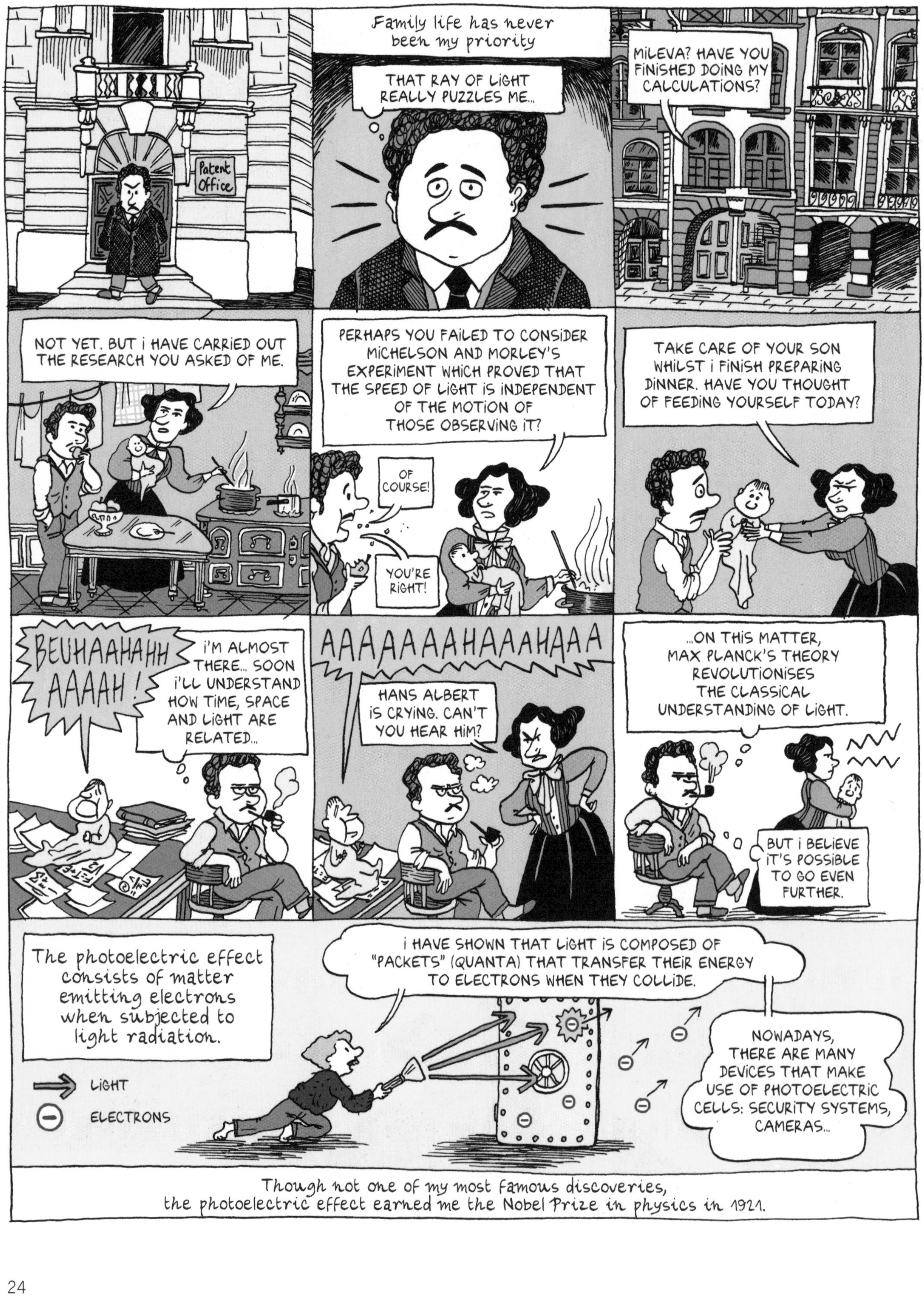

Patent Office
Family life has never been my priority
THAT RAY OF LIGHT REALLY PUZZLES ME...
MILEVA? HAVE YOU FINISHED DOING MY CALCULATIONS?
NOT YET. BUT I HAVE CARRIED OUT THE RESEARCH YOU ASKED OF ME.
PERHAPS YOU FAILED TO CONSIDER MICHELSON AND MORLEY'S EXPERIMENT WHICH PROVED THAT THE SPEED OF LIGHT IS INDEPENDENT OF THE MOTION OF THOSE OBSERVING IT?
OF COURSE!
YOU'RE RIGHT!
TAKE CARE OF YOUR SON WHILST I FINISH PREPARING DINNER. HAVE YOU THOUGHT OF FEEDING YOURSELF TODAY?
BEUHAAAHAHH AAAAH!
I'M ALMOST THERE... SOON I'LL UNDERSTAND HOW TIME, SPACE AND LIGHT ARE RELATED...
AAAAAAAHAAAHAAA
HANS ALBERT IS CRYING. CAN'T YOU HEAR HIM?
...ON THIS MATTER, MAX PLANCK'S THEORY REVOLUTIONISES THE CLASSICAL UNDERSTANDING OF LIGHT.
BUT I BELIEVE IT'S POSSIBLE TO GO EVEN FURTHER.
The photoelectric effect consists of matter emitting electrons when subjected to light radiation.
I HAVE SHOWN THAT LIGHT IS COMPOSED OF "PACKETS" (QUANTA) THAT TRANSFER THEIR ENERGY TO ELECTRONS WHEN THEY COLLIDE.
LIGHT
ELECTRONS
NOWADAYS, THERE ARE MANY DEVICES THAT MAKE USE OF PHOTOELECTRIC CELLS: SECURITY SYSTEMS, CAMERAS...
Though not one of my most famous discoveries, the photoelectric effect earned me the Nobel Prize in physics in 1921.

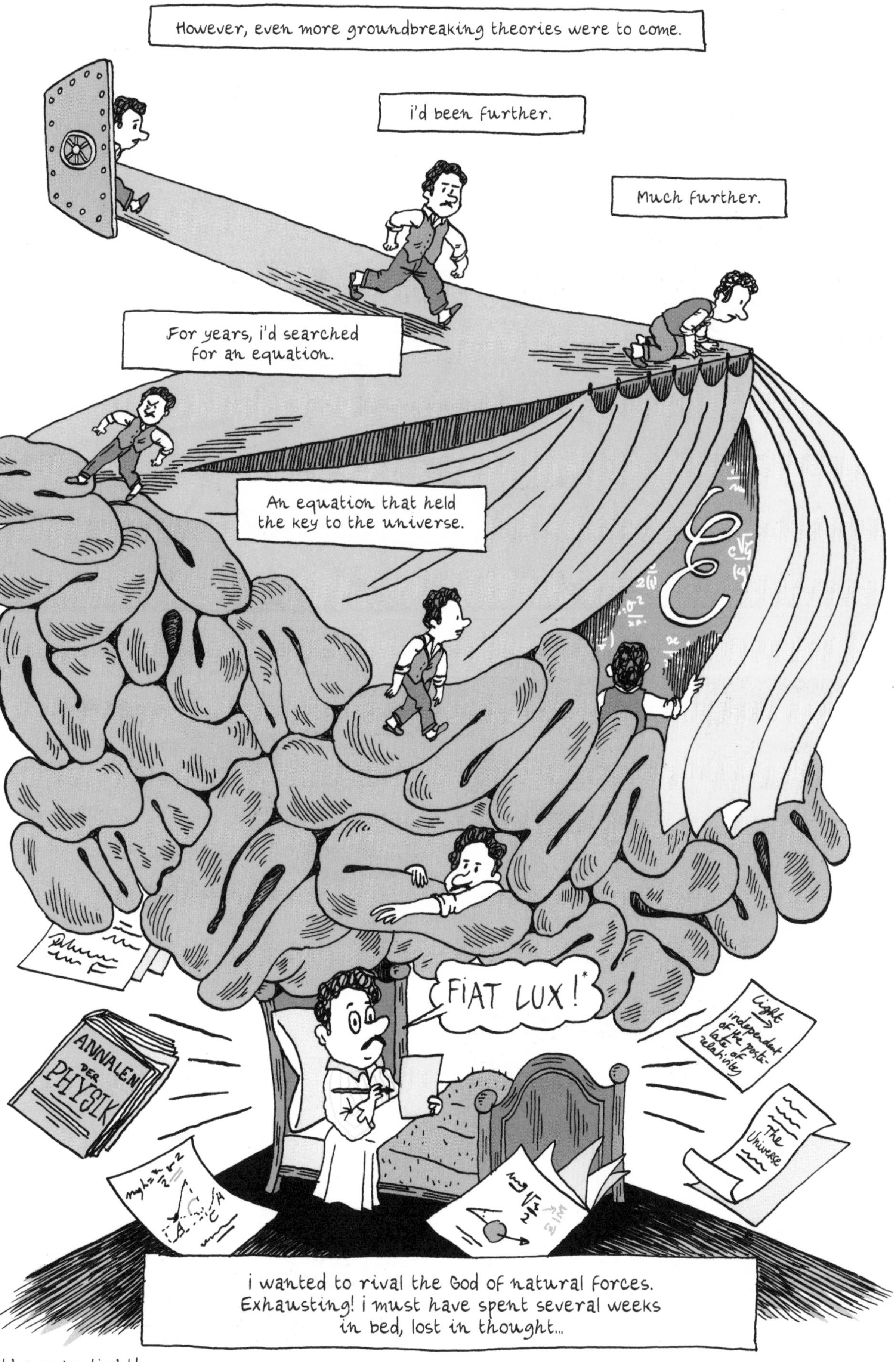
However, even more groundbreaking theories were to come.
i'd been further.
Much further.
For years, i'd searched for an equation.
An equation that held the key to the universe.
FIAT LUX!*
ANNALEN DER PHYSIK
Light → independent of the postulate of relativity
The Universe
i wanted to rival the God of natural forces. Exhausting! i must have spent several weeks in bed, lost in thought...

* Let there be light!

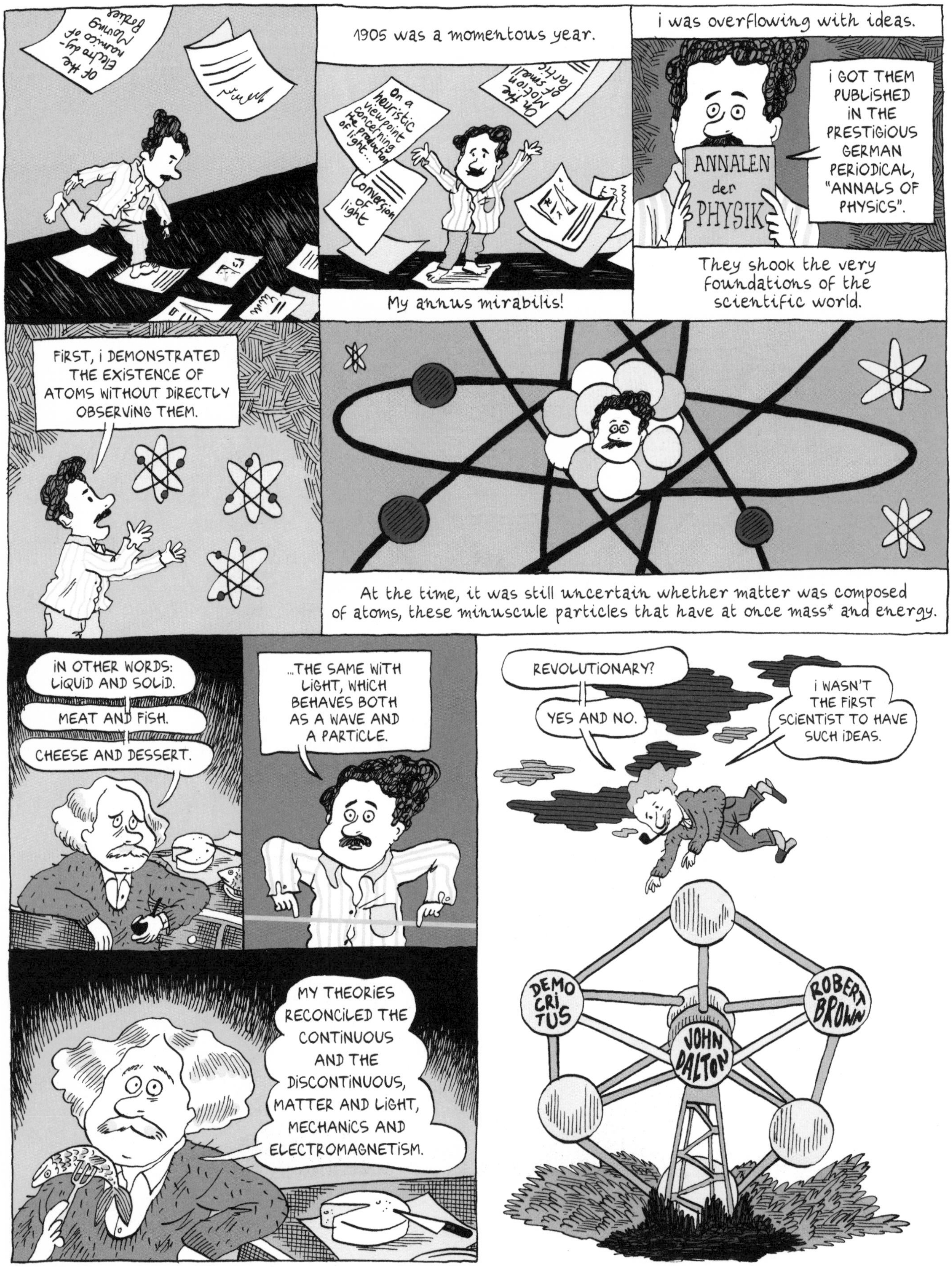
1905 was a momentous year.
On a heuristic viewpoint concerning the production of light...
Conversion of light
My annus mirabilis!
i was overflowing with ideas.
ANNALEN der PHYSIK
i GOT THEM PUBLiSHED iN THE PRESTiGiOUS GERMAN PERiODiCAL, "ANNALS OF PHYSiCS".
They shook the very foundations of the scientific world.
FiRST, i DEMONSTRATED THE EXiSTENCE OF ATOMS WiTHOUT DiRECTLY OBSERViNG THEM.
At the time, it was still uncertain whether matter was composed of atoms, these minuscule particles that have at once mass* and energy.
iN OTHER WORDS: LiQUiD AND SOLiD.
MEAT AND FiSH.
CHEESE AND DESSERT.
...THE SAME WiTH LiGHT, WHiCH BEHAVES BOTH AS A WAVE AND A PARTiCLE.
MY THEORiES RECONCiLED THE CONTiNUOUS AND THE DiSCONTiNUOUS, MATTER AND LiGHT, MECHANiCS AND ELECTROMAGNETiSM.
REVOLUTiONARY?
YES AND NO.
i WASN'T THE FiRST SCiENTiST TO HAVE SUCH iDEAS.
DEMOCRiTUS
ROBERT BROWN
JOHN DALTON

* Quantity of matter in a body.

THE THEORY OF SPECIAL RELATIVITY

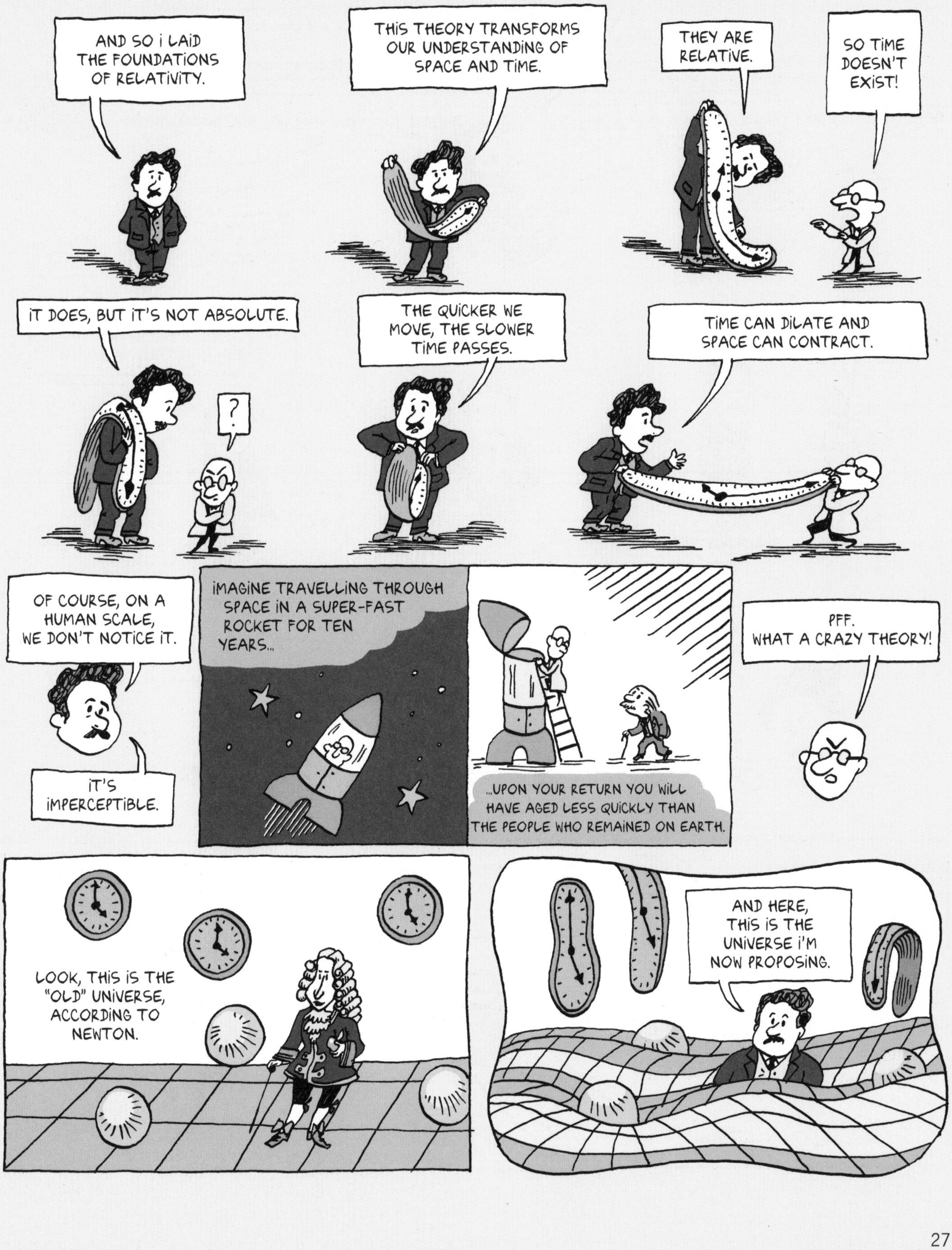
AND SO I LAID THE FOUNDATIONS OF RELATIVITY.
THIS THEORY TRANSFORMS OUR UNDERSTANDING OF SPACE AND TIME.
THEY ARE RELATIVE.
SO TIME DOESN'T EXIST!
IT DOES, BUT IT'S NOT ABSOLUTE.
?
THE QUICKER WE MOVE, THE SLOWER TIME PASSES.
TIME CAN DILATE AND SPACE CAN CONTRACT.
OF COURSE, ON A HUMAN SCALE, WE DON'T NOTICE IT.
IT'S IMPERCEPTIBLE.
IMAGINE TRAVELLING THROUGH SPACE IN A SUPER-FAST ROCKET FOR TEN YEARS...
...UPON YOUR RETURN YOU WILL HAVE AGED LESS QUICKLY THAN THE PEOPLE WHO REMAINED ON EARTH.
PFF. WHAT A CRAZY THEORY!
LOOK, THIS IS THE "OLD" UNIVERSE, ACCORDING TO NEWTON.
AND HERE, THIS IS THE UNIVERSE I'M NOW PROPOSING.

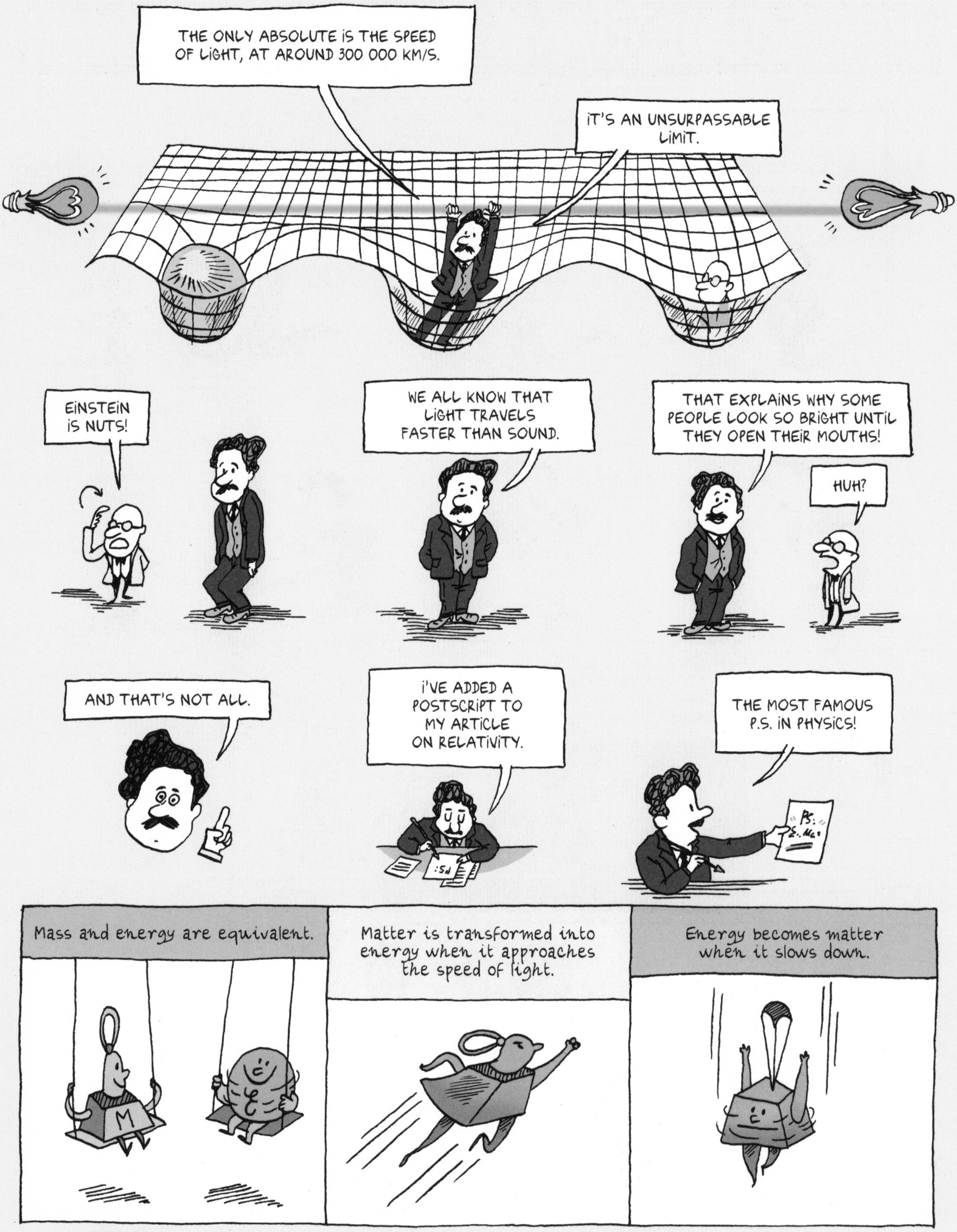
THE ONLY ABSOLUTE IS THE SPEED OF LIGHT, AT AROUND 300 000 KM/S.
IT'S AN UNSURPASSABLE LIMIT.
EINSTEIN IS NUTS!
WE ALL KNOW THAT LIGHT TRAVELS FASTER THAN SOUND.
THAT EXPLAINS WHY SOME PEOPLE LOOK SO BRIGHT UNTIL THEY OPEN THEIR MOUTHS!
HUH?
AND THAT'S NOT ALL.
I'VE ADDED A POSTSCRIPT TO MY ARTICLE ON RELATIVITY.
THE MOST FAMOUS P.S. IN PHYSICS!
Mass and energy are equivalent.
Matter is transformed into energy when it approaches the speed of light.
Energy becomes matter when it slows down.

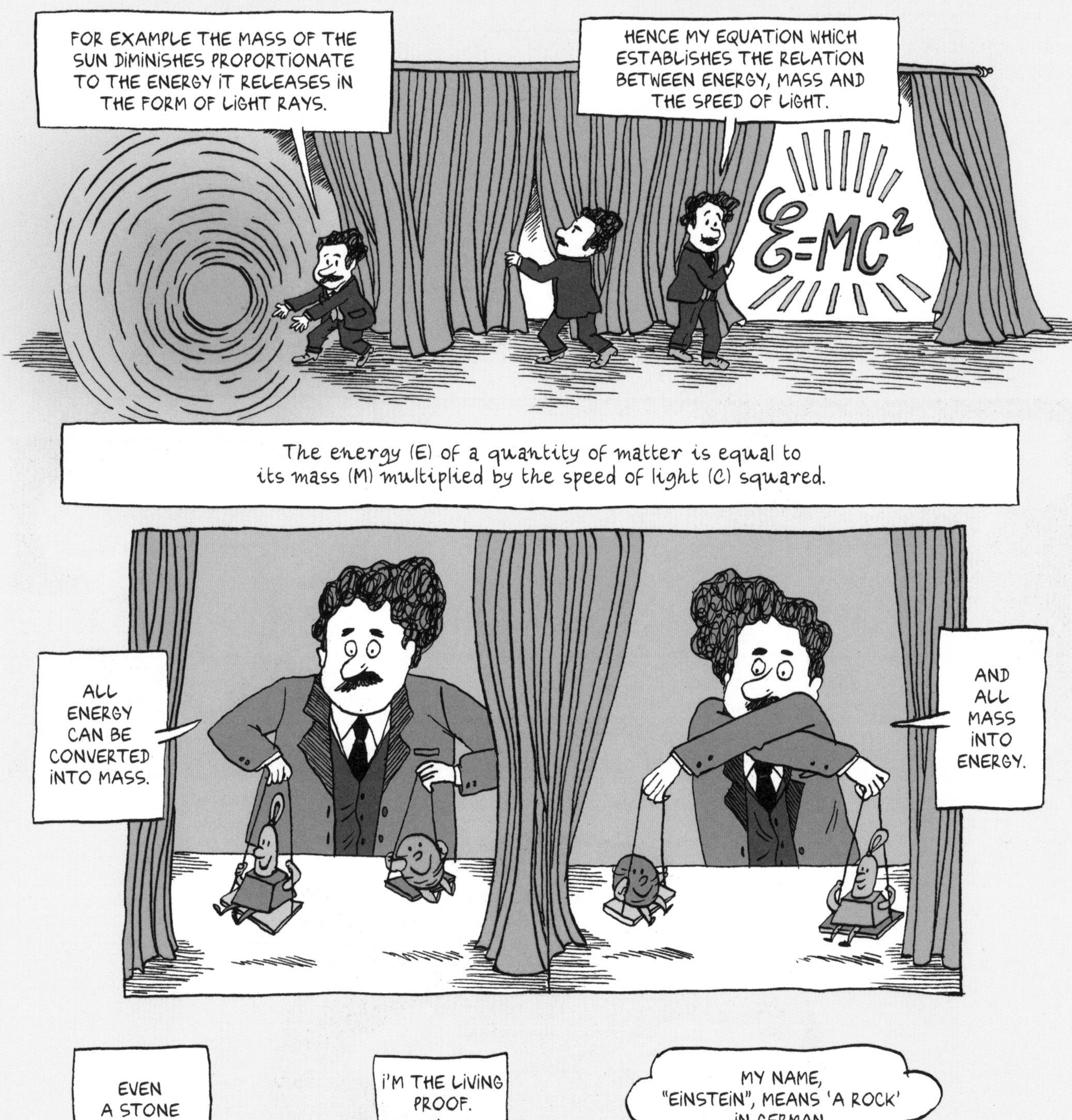
FOR EXAMPLE THE MASS OF THE SUN DIMINISHES PROPORTIONATE TO THE ENERGY IT RELEASES IN THE FORM OF LIGHT RAYS.
HENCE MY EQUATION WHICH ESTABLISHES THE RELATION BETWEEN ENERGY, MASS AND THE SPEED OF LIGHT.
E=MC²
The energy (E) of a quantity of matter is equal to its mass (M) multiplied by the speed of light (C) squared.
ALL ENERGY CAN BE CONVERTED INTO MASS.
AND ALL MASS INTO ENERGY.
EVEN A STONE HAS ENERGY.
I'M THE LIVING PROOF.
MY NAME, "EINSTEIN", MEANS 'A ROCK' IN GERMAN.

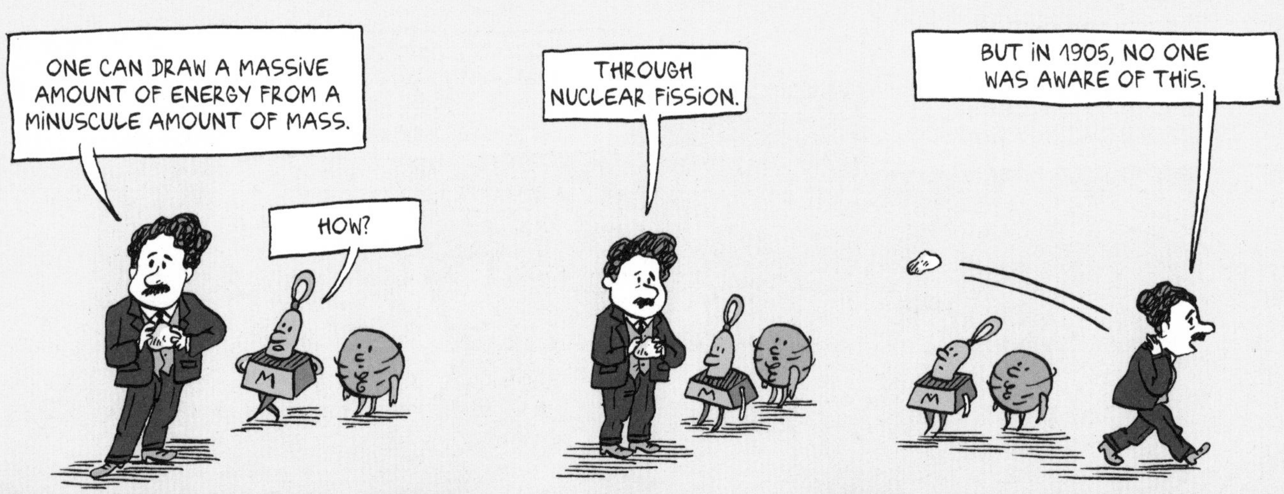
ONE CAN DRAW A MASSIVE AMOUNT OF ENERGY FROM A MINUSCULE AMOUNT OF MASS.
HOW?
THROUGH NUCLEAR FISSION.
BUT IN 1905, NO ONE WAS AWARE OF THIS.

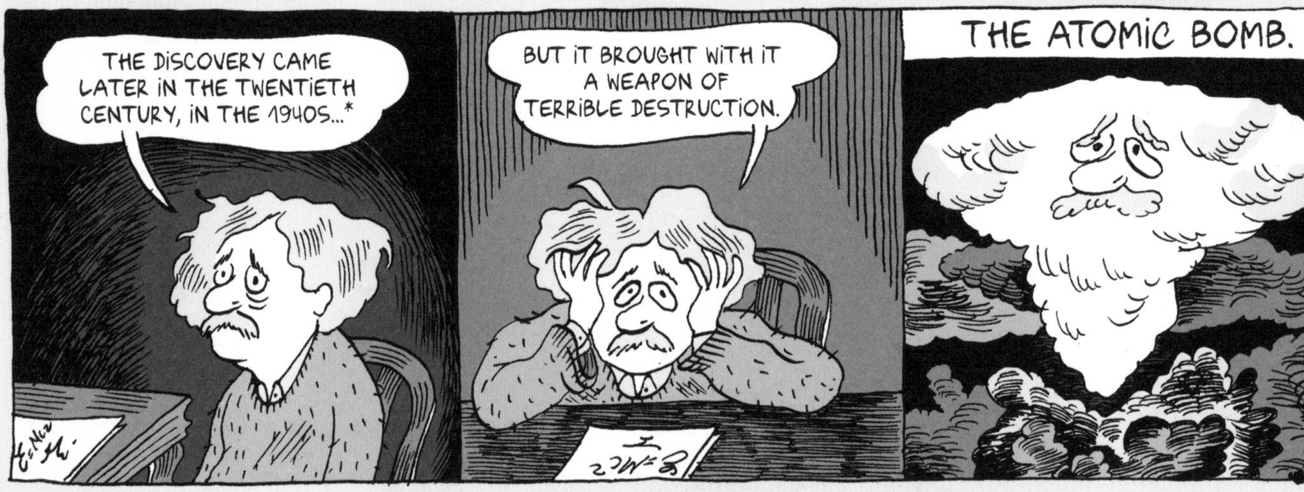
THE DISCOVERY CAME LATER IN THE TWENTIETH CENTURY, IN THE 1940S...*
BUT IT BROUGHT WITH IT A WEAPON OF TERRIBLE DESTRUCTION.
THE ATOMIC BOMB.

*Nuclear physics was developed by Joliot - Curie, Fermi, Meitner and Szilárd.

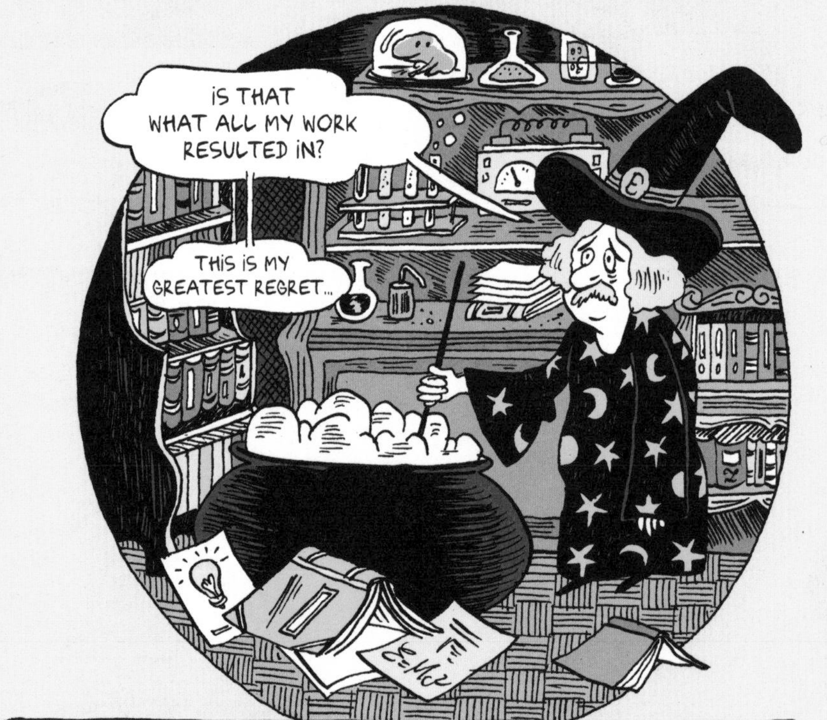
IS THAT WHAT ALL MY WORK RESULTED IN?
THIS IS MY GREATEST REGRET...
Had i known, believe me, i would have become a cobbler.

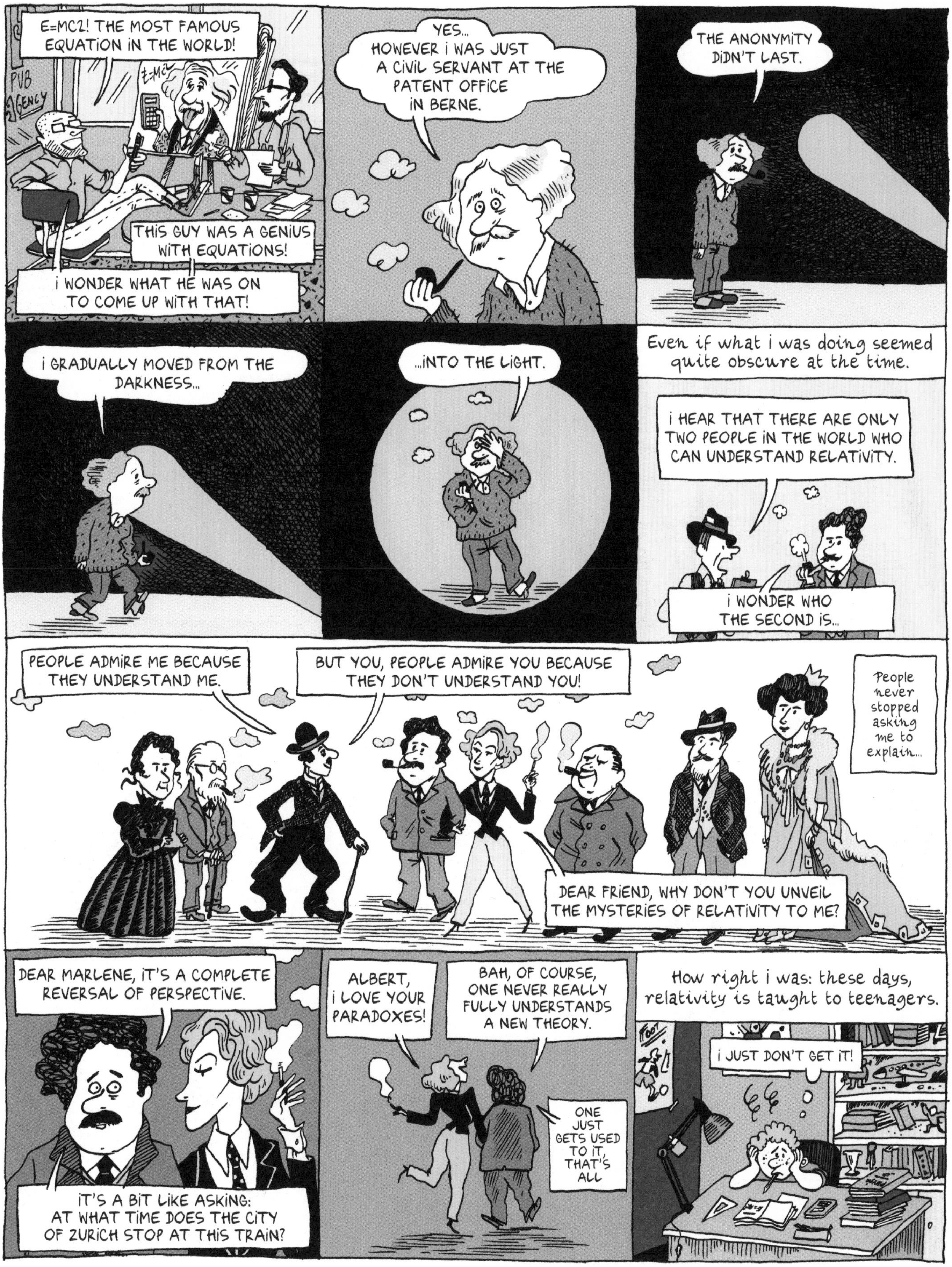
E=MC2! THE MOST FAMOUS EQUATION IN THE WORLD!
PUB AGENCY
THIS GUY WAS A GENIUS WITH EQUATIONS!
I WONDER WHAT HE WAS ON TO COME UP WITH THAT!
YES... HOWEVER I WAS JUST A CIVIL SERVANT AT THE PATENT OFFICE IN BERNE.
THE ANONYMITY DIDN'T LAST.
I GRADUALLY MOVED FROM THE DARKNESS...
...INTO THE LIGHT.
Even if what I was doing seemed quite obscure at the time.
I HEAR THAT THERE ARE ONLY TWO PEOPLE IN THE WORLD WHO CAN UNDERSTAND RELATIVITY.
I WONDER WHO THE SECOND IS...
PEOPLE ADMIRE ME BECAUSE THEY UNDERSTAND ME.
BUT YOU, PEOPLE ADMIRE YOU BECAUSE THEY DON'T UNDERSTAND YOU!
People never stopped asking me to explain...
DEAR FRIEND, WHY DON'T YOU UNVEIL THE MYSTERIES OF RELATIVITY TO ME?
DEAR MARLENE, IT'S A COMPLETE REVERSAL OF PERSPECTIVE.
IT'S A BIT LIKE ASKING: AT WHAT TIME DOES THE CITY OF ZURICH STOP AT THIS TRAIN?
ALBERT, I LOVE YOUR PARADOXES!
BAH, OF COURSE, ONE NEVER REALLY FULLY UNDERSTANDS A NEW THEORY.
ONE JUST GETS USED TO IT, THAT'S ALL
How right I was: these days, relativity is taught to teenagers.
I JUST DON'T GET IT!

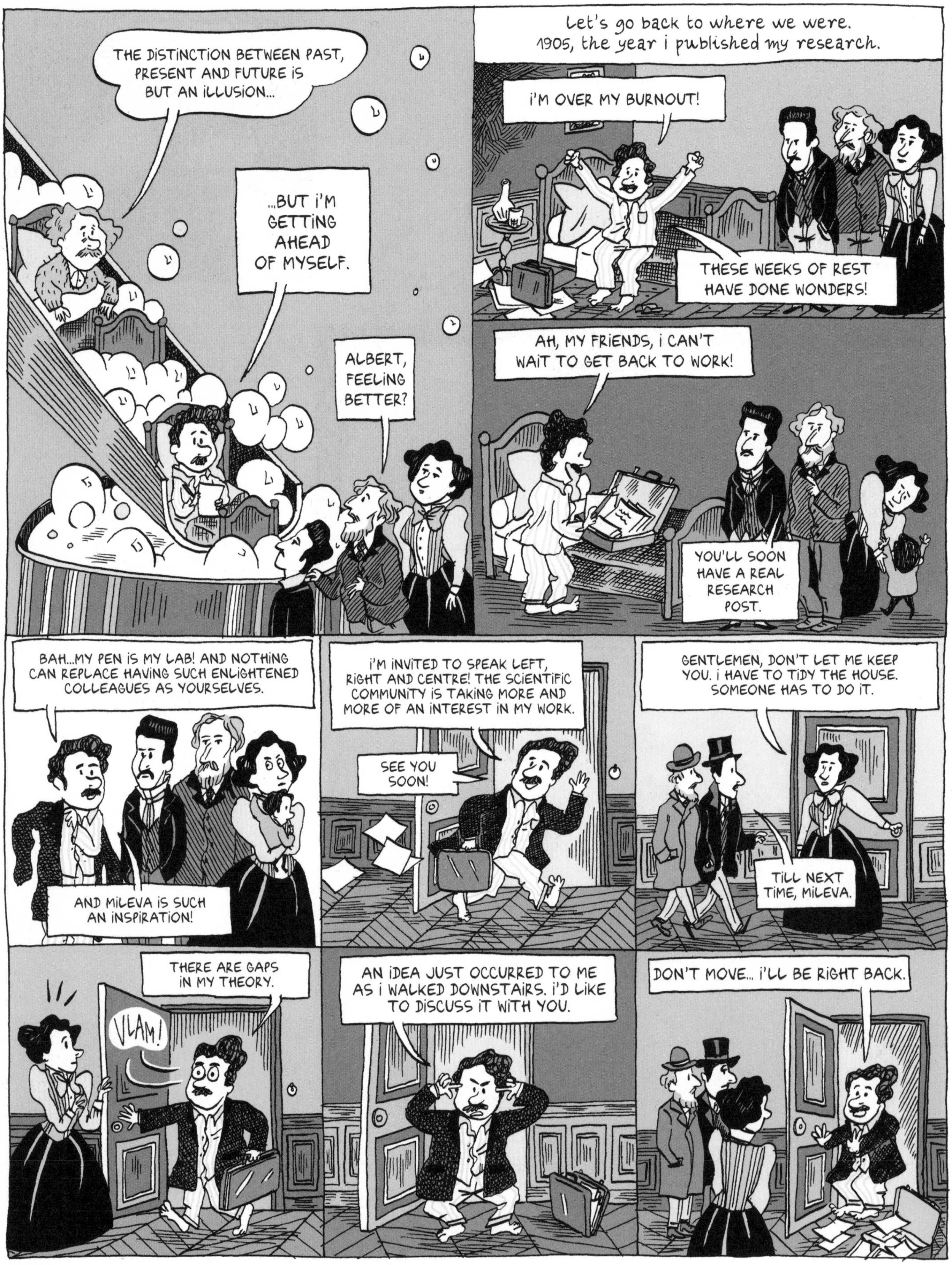
THE DISTINCTION BETWEEN PAST, PRESENT AND FUTURE IS BUT AN ILLUSION...
...BUT I'M GETTING AHEAD OF MYSELF.
ALBERT, FEELING BETTER?
Let's go back to where we were. 1905, the year I published my research.
I'M OVER MY BURNOUT!
THESE WEEKS OF REST HAVE DONE WONDERS!
AH, MY FRIENDS, I CAN'T WAIT TO GET BACK TO WORK!
YOU'LL SOON HAVE A REAL RESEARCH POST.
BAH...MY PEN IS MY LAB! AND NOTHING CAN REPLACE HAVING SUCH ENLIGHTENED COLLEAGUES AS YOURSELVES.
AND MILEVA IS SUCH AN INSPIRATION!
I'M INVITED TO SPEAK LEFT, RIGHT AND CENTRE! THE SCIENTIFIC COMMUNITY IS TAKING MORE AND MORE OF AN INTEREST IN MY WORK.
SEE YOU SOON!
GENTLEMEN, DON'T LET ME KEEP YOU. I HAVE TO TIDY THE HOUSE. SOMEONE HAS TO DO IT.
TILL NEXT TIME, MILEVA.
THERE ARE GAPS IN MY THEORY.
VLAM!
AN IDEA JUST OCCURRED TO ME AS I WALKED DOWNSTAIRS. I'D LIKE TO DISCUSS IT WITH YOU.
DON'T MOVE... I'LL BE RIGHT BACK.

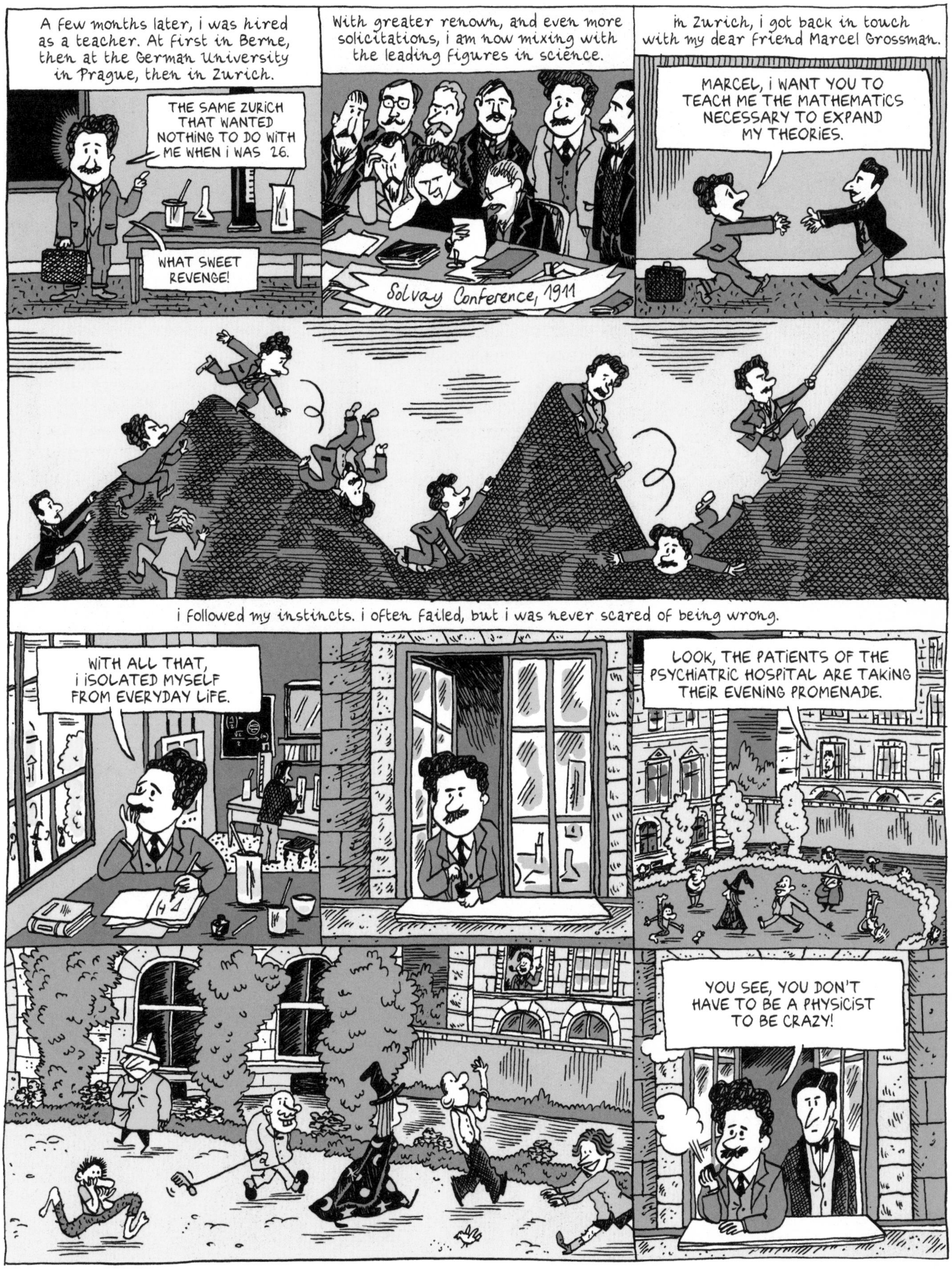
A few months later, i was hired as a teacher. At first in Berne, then at the German University in Prague, then in Zurich.
THE SAME ZURICH THAT WANTED NOTHING TO DO WITH ME WHEN i WAS 26.
WHAT SWEET REVENGE!
With greater renown, and even more solicitations, i am now mixing with the leading figures in science.
Solvay Conference, 1911
in Zurich, i got back in touch with my dear friend Marcel Grossman.
MARCEL, i WANT YOU TO TEACH ME THE MATHEMATICS NECESSARY TO EXPAND MY THEORIES.
i followed my instincts. i often failed, but i was never scared of being wrong.
WiTH ALL THAT, i iSOLATED MYSELF FROM EVERYDAY LiFE.
LOOK, THE PATiENTS OF THE PSYCHiATRiC HOSPiTAL ARE TAKiNG THEiR EVENiNG PROMENADE.
YOU SEE, YOU DON'T HAVE TO BE A PHYSiCiST TO BE CRAZY!

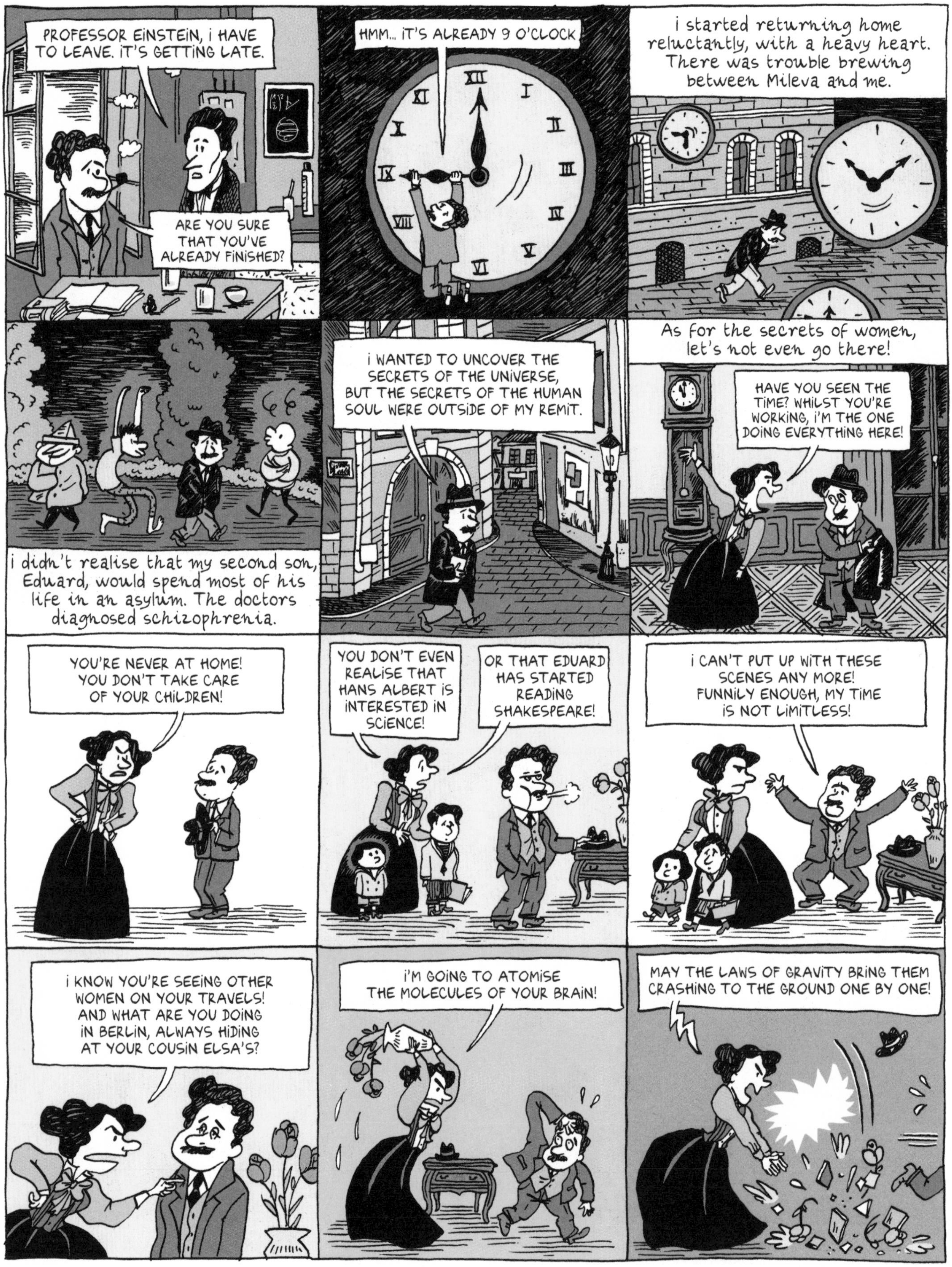
PROFESSOR EINSTEIN, I HAVE TO LEAVE. IT'S GETTING LATE.
ARE YOU SURE THAT YOU'VE ALREADY FINISHED?
HMM... IT'S ALREADY 9 O'CLOCK
I started returning home reluctantly, with a heavy heart. There was trouble brewing between Mileva and me.
I didn't realise that my second son, Eduard, would spend most of his life in an asylum. The doctors diagnosed schizophrenia.
I WANTED TO UNCOVER THE SECRETS OF THE UNIVERSE, BUT THE SECRETS OF THE HUMAN SOUL WERE OUTSIDE OF MY REMIT.
As for the secrets of women, let's not even go there!
HAVE YOU SEEN THE TIME? WHILST YOU'RE WORKING, I'M THE ONE DOING EVERYTHING HERE!
YOU'RE NEVER AT HOME! YOU DON'T TAKE CARE OF YOUR CHILDREN!
YOU DON'T EVEN REALISE THAT HANS ALBERT IS INTERESTED IN SCIENCE!
OR THAT EDUARD HAS STARTED READING SHAKESPEARE!
I CAN'T PUT UP WITH THESE SCENES ANY MORE! FUNNILY ENOUGH, MY TIME IS NOT LIMITLESS!
I KNOW YOU'RE SEEING OTHER WOMEN ON YOUR TRAVELS! AND WHAT ARE YOU DOING IN BERLIN, ALWAYS HIDING AT YOUR COUSIN ELSA'S?
I'M GOING TO ATOMISE THE MOLECULES OF YOUR BRAIN!
MAY THE LAWS OF GRAVITY BRING THEM CRASHING TO THE GROUND ONE BY ONE!

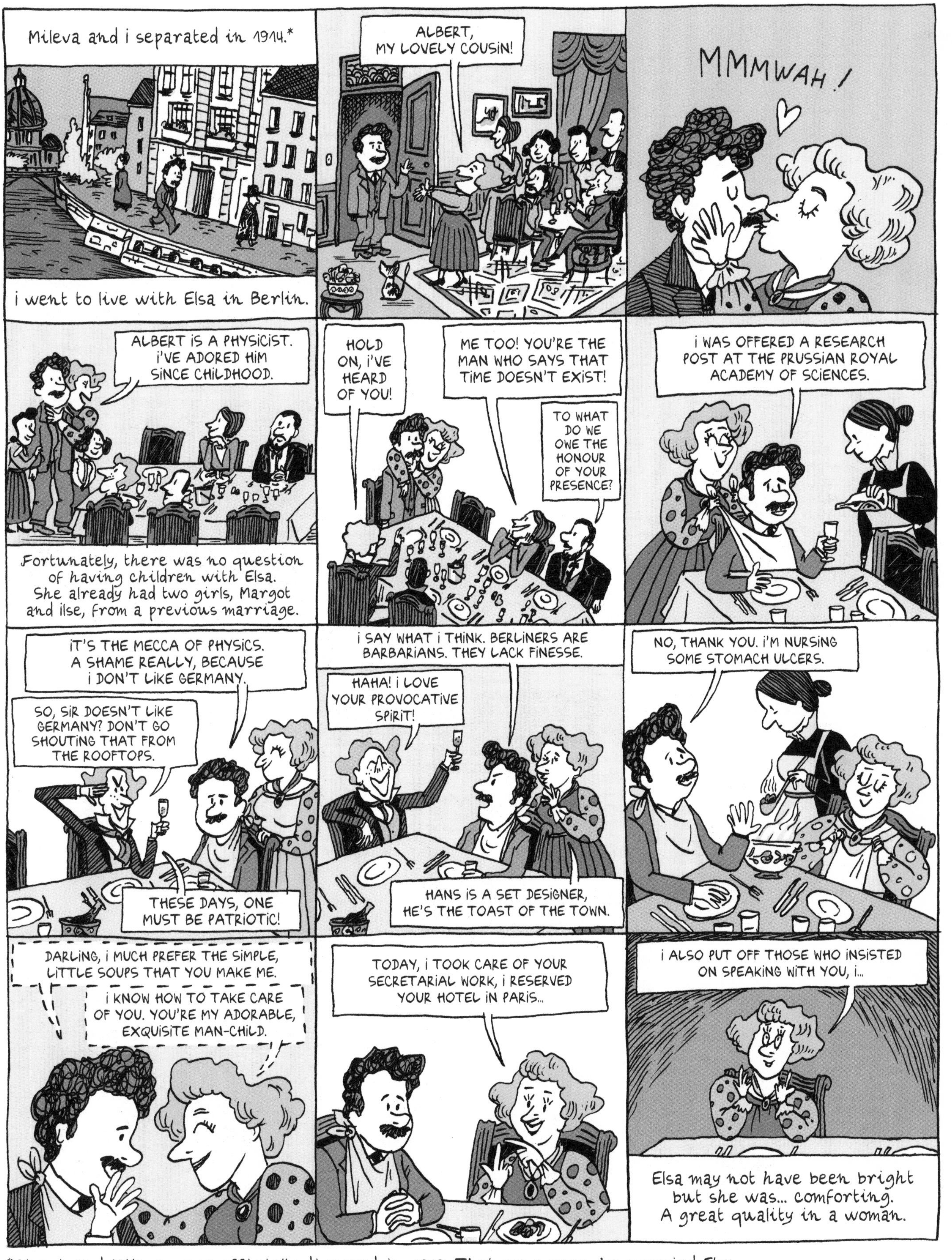

Mileva and i separated in 1914.*
i went to live with Elsa in Berlin.
ALBERT, MY LOVELY COUSIN!
MMMWAH!
ALBERT IS A PHYSICIST. i'VE ADORED HIM SINCE CHILDHOOD.
Fortunately, there was no question of having children with Elsa. She already had two girls, Margot and ilse, from a previous marriage.
HOLD ON, i'VE HEARD OF YOU!
ME TOO! YOU'RE THE MAN WHO SAYS THAT TIME DOESN'T EXIST!
TO WHAT DO WE OWE THE HONOUR OF YOUR PRESENCE?
i WAS OFFERED A RESEARCH POST AT THE PRUSSIAN ROYAL ACADEMY OF SCIENCES.
iT'S THE MECCA OF PHYSICS. A SHAME REALLY, BECAUSE i DON'T LIKE GERMANY.
SO, SIR DOESN'T LIKE GERMANY? DON'T GO SHOUTING THAT FROM THE ROOFTOPS.
THESE DAYS, ONE MUST BE PATRIOTIC!
i SAY WHAT i THINK. BERLINERS ARE BARBARIANS. THEY LACK FINESSE.
HAHA! i LOVE YOUR PROVOCATIVE SPIRIT!
HANS IS A SET DESIGNER, HE'S THE TOAST OF THE TOWN.
NO, THANK YOU. i'M NURSING SOME STOMACH ULCERS.
DARLING, i MUCH PREFER THE SIMPLE, LITTLE SOUPS THAT YOU MAKE ME.
i KNOW HOW TO TAKE CARE OF YOU. YOU'RE MY ADORABLE, EXQUISITE MAN-CHILD.
TODAY, i TOOK CARE OF YOUR SECRETARIAL WORK, i RESERVED YOUR HOTEL iN PARIS...
i ALSO PUT OFF THOSE WHO INSISTED ON SPEAKING WITH YOU, i...
Elsa may not have been bright but she was... comforting. A great quality in a woman.

*Albert and Mileva were officially divorced in 1919. That same year, he married Elsa.

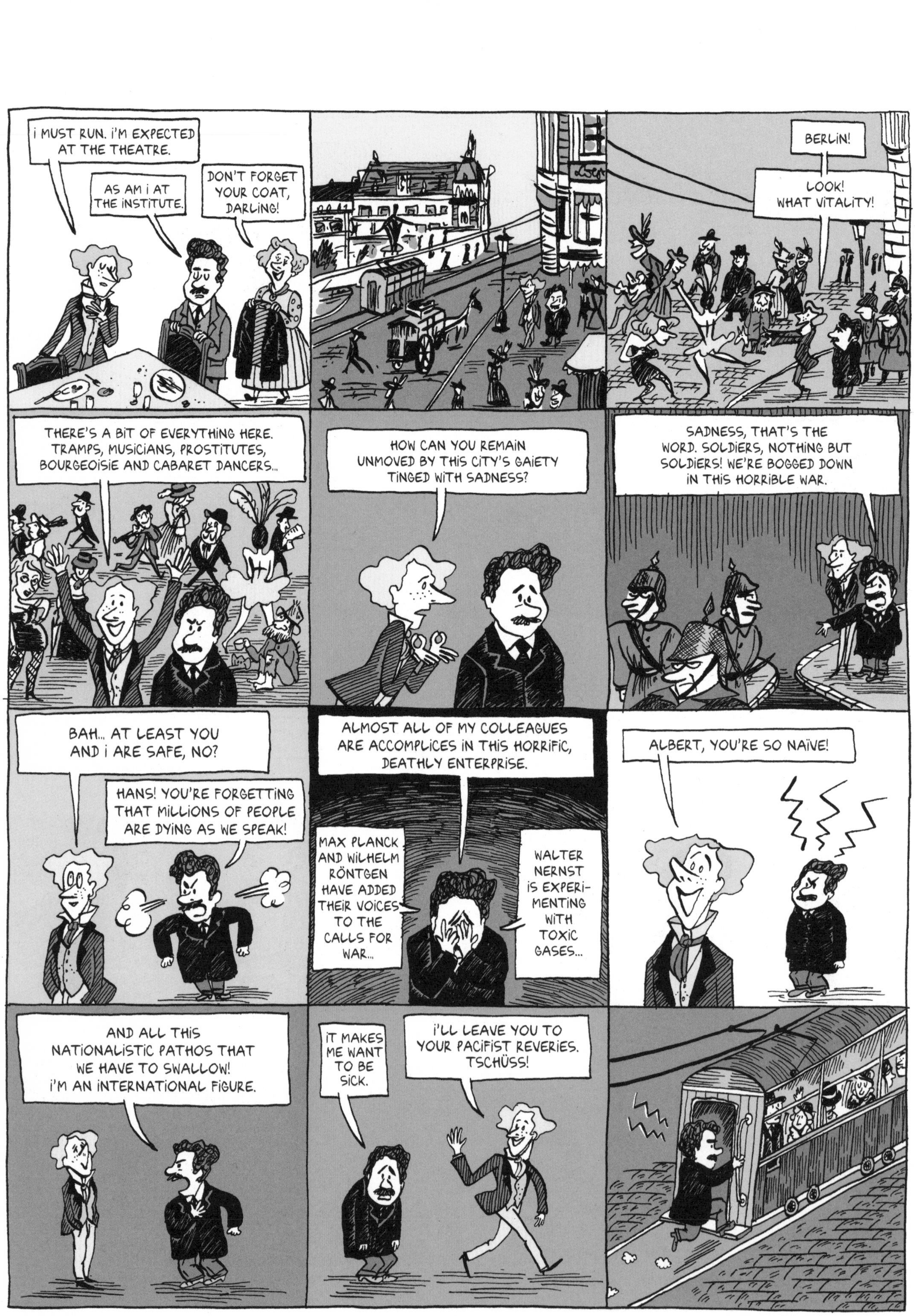
I MUST RUN. I'M EXPECTED AT THE THEATRE.
AS AM I AT THE INSTITUTE.
DON'T FORGET YOUR COAT, DARLING!
BERLIN!
LOOK! WHAT VITALITY!
THERE'S A BIT OF EVERYTHING HERE. TRAMPS, MUSICIANS, PROSTITUTES, BOURGEOISIE AND CABARET DANCERS...
HOW CAN YOU REMAIN UNMOVED BY THIS CITY'S GAIETY TINGED WITH SADNESS?
SADNESS, THAT'S THE WORD. SOLDIERS, NOTHING BUT SOLDIERS! WE'RE BOGGED DOWN IN THIS HORRIBLE WAR.
BAH... AT LEAST YOU AND I ARE SAFE, NO?
HANS! YOU'RE FORGETTING THAT MILLIONS OF PEOPLE ARE DYING AS WE SPEAK!
ALMOST ALL OF MY COLLEAGUES ARE ACCOMPLICES IN THIS HORRIFIC, DEATHLY ENTERPRISE.
MAX PLANCK AND WILHELM RÖNTGEN HAVE ADDED THEIR VOICES TO THE CALLS FOR WAR...
WALTER NERNST IS EXPERI-MENTING WITH TOXIC GASES...
ALBERT, YOU'RE SO NAÏVE!
AND ALL THIS NATIONALISTIC PATHOS THAT WE HAVE TO SWALLOW! I'M AN INTERNATIONAL FIGURE.
IT MAKES ME WANT TO BE SICK.
I'LL LEAVE YOU TO YOUR PACIFIST REVERIES. TSCHÜSS!

THE THEORY OF GENERAL RELATIVITY

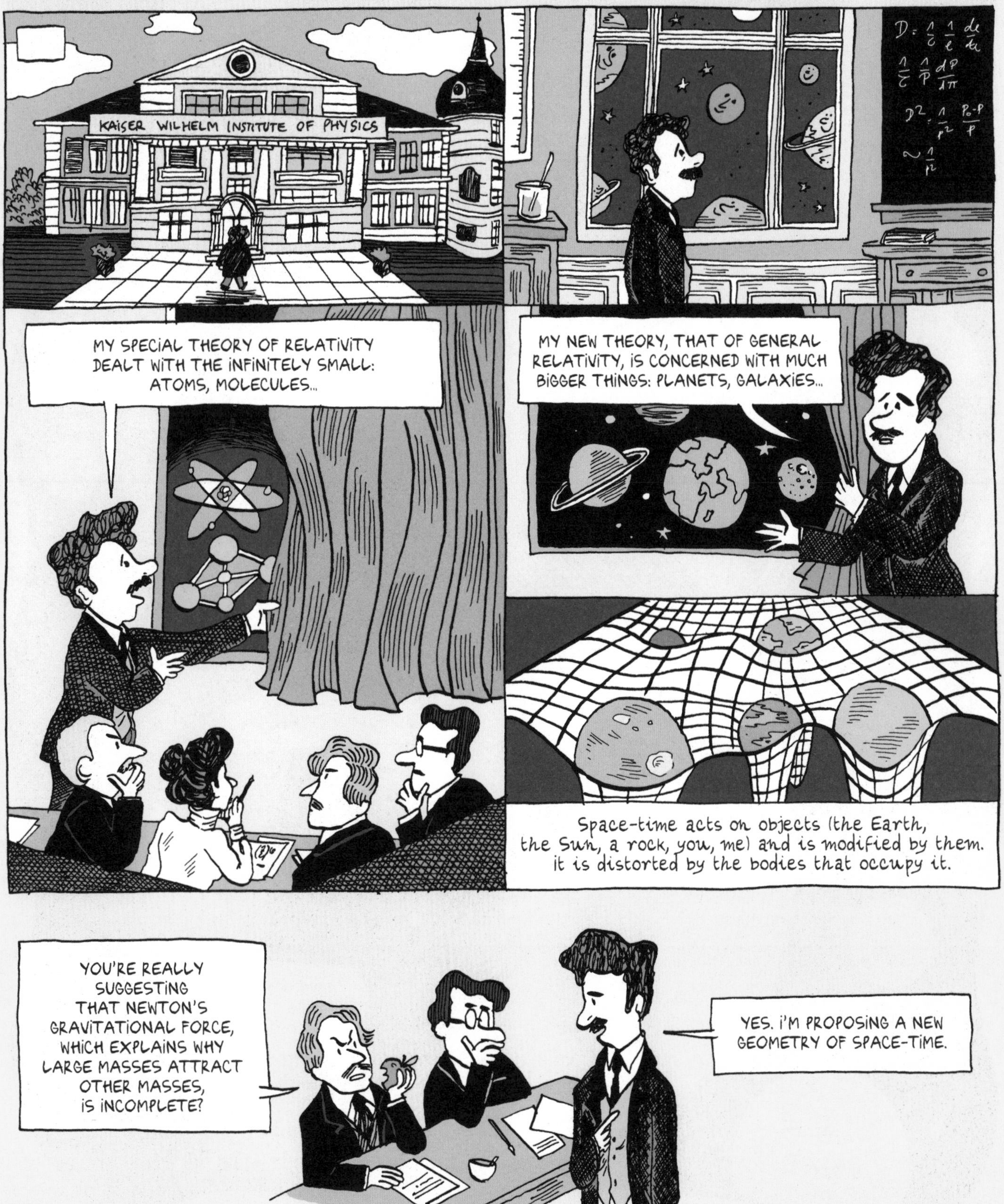
KAISER WILHELM INSTITUTE OF PHYSICS
MY SPECIAL THEORY OF RELATIVITY DEALT WITH THE INFINITELY SMALL: ATOMS, MOLECULES...
MY NEW THEORY, THAT OF GENERAL RELATIVITY, IS CONCERNED WITH MUCH BIGGER THINGS: PLANETS, GALAXIES...
Space-time acts on objects (the Earth, the Sun, a rock, you, me) and is modified by them. It is distorted by the bodies that occupy it.
YOU'RE REALLY SUGGESTING THAT NEWTON'S GRAVITATIONAL FORCE, WHICH EXPLAINS WHY LARGE MASSES ATTRACT OTHER MASSES, IS INCOMPLETE?
YES. I'M PROPOSING A NEW GEOMETRY OF SPACE-TIME.

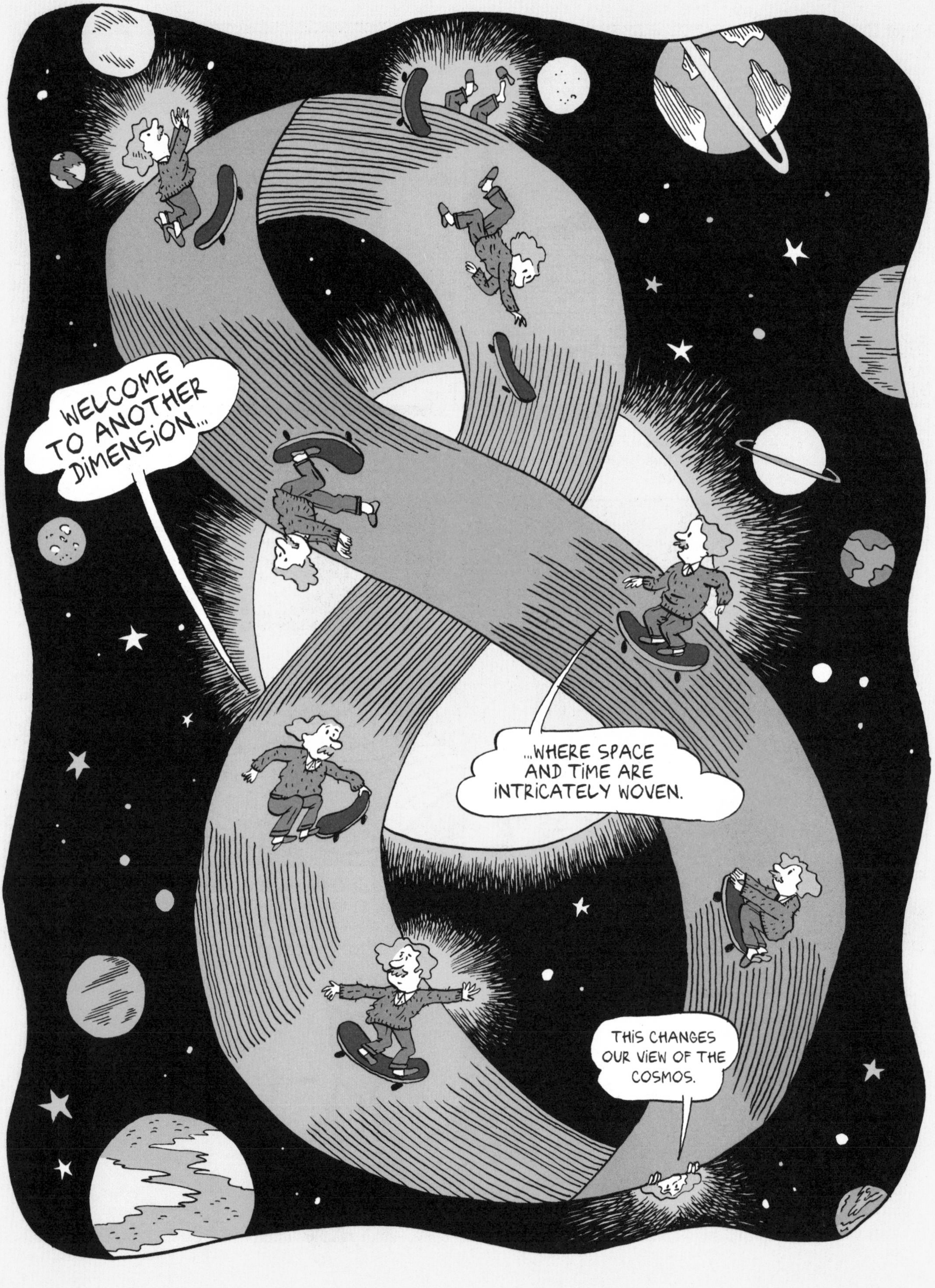
WELCOME TO ANOTHER DIMENSION...
...WHERE SPACE AND TIME ARE INTRICATELY WOVEN.
THIS CHANGES OUR VIEW OF THE COSMOS.

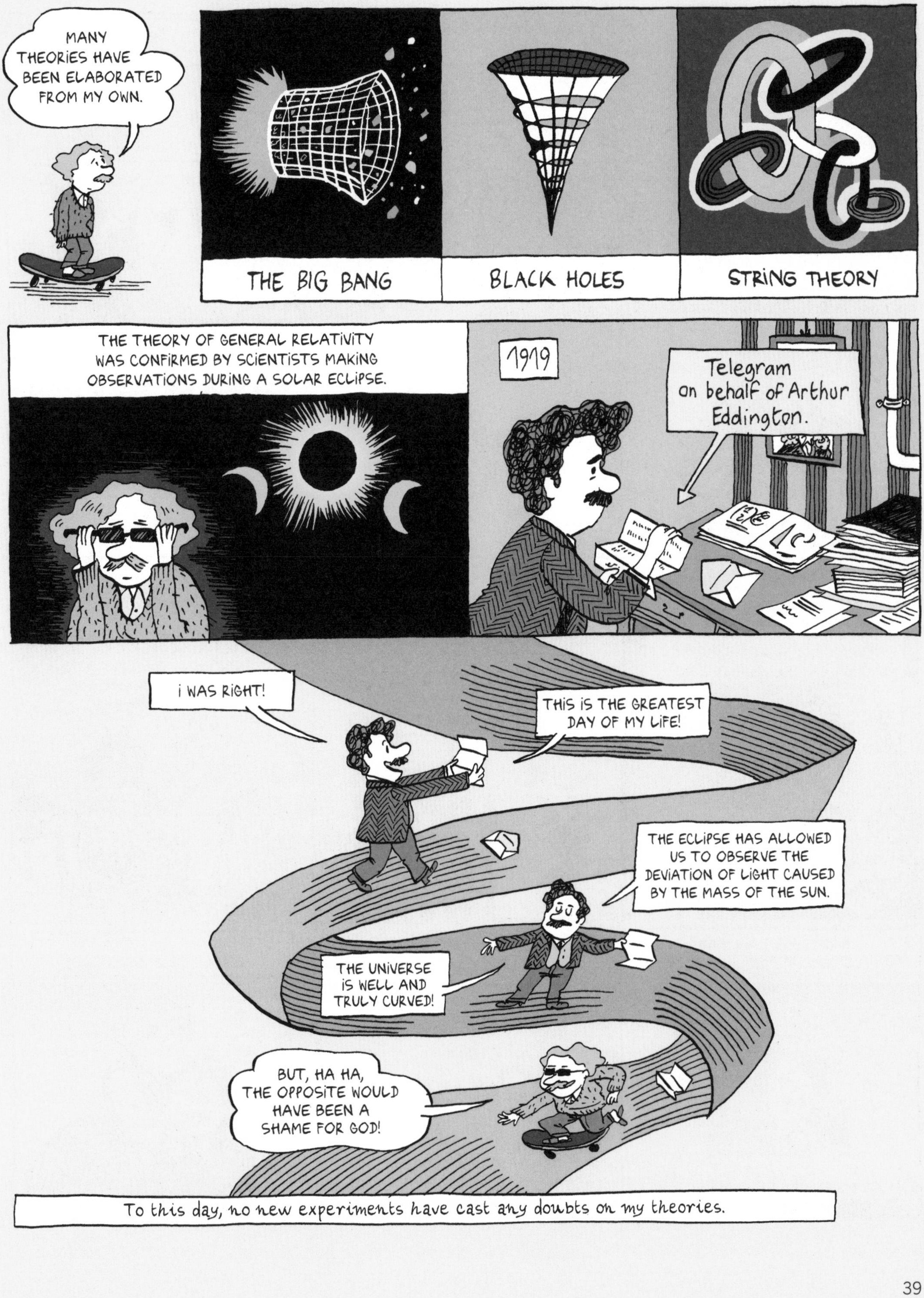
MANY THEORIES HAVE BEEN ELABORATED FROM MY OWN.
THE BIG BANG
BLACK HOLES
STRING THEORY
THE THEORY OF GENERAL RELATIVITY WAS CONFIRMED BY SCIENTISTS MAKING OBSERVATIONS DURING A SOLAR ECLIPSE.
1919
Telegram on behalf of Arthur Eddington.
I WAS RIGHT!
THIS IS THE GREATEST DAY OF MY LIFE!
THE ECLIPSE HAS ALLOWED US TO OBSERVE THE DEVIATION OF LIGHT CAUSED BY THE MASS OF THE SUN.
THE UNIVERSE IS WELL AND TRULY CURVED!
BUT, HA HA, THE OPPOSITE WOULD HAVE BEEN A SHAME FOR GOD!
To this day, no new experiments have cast any doubts on my theories.

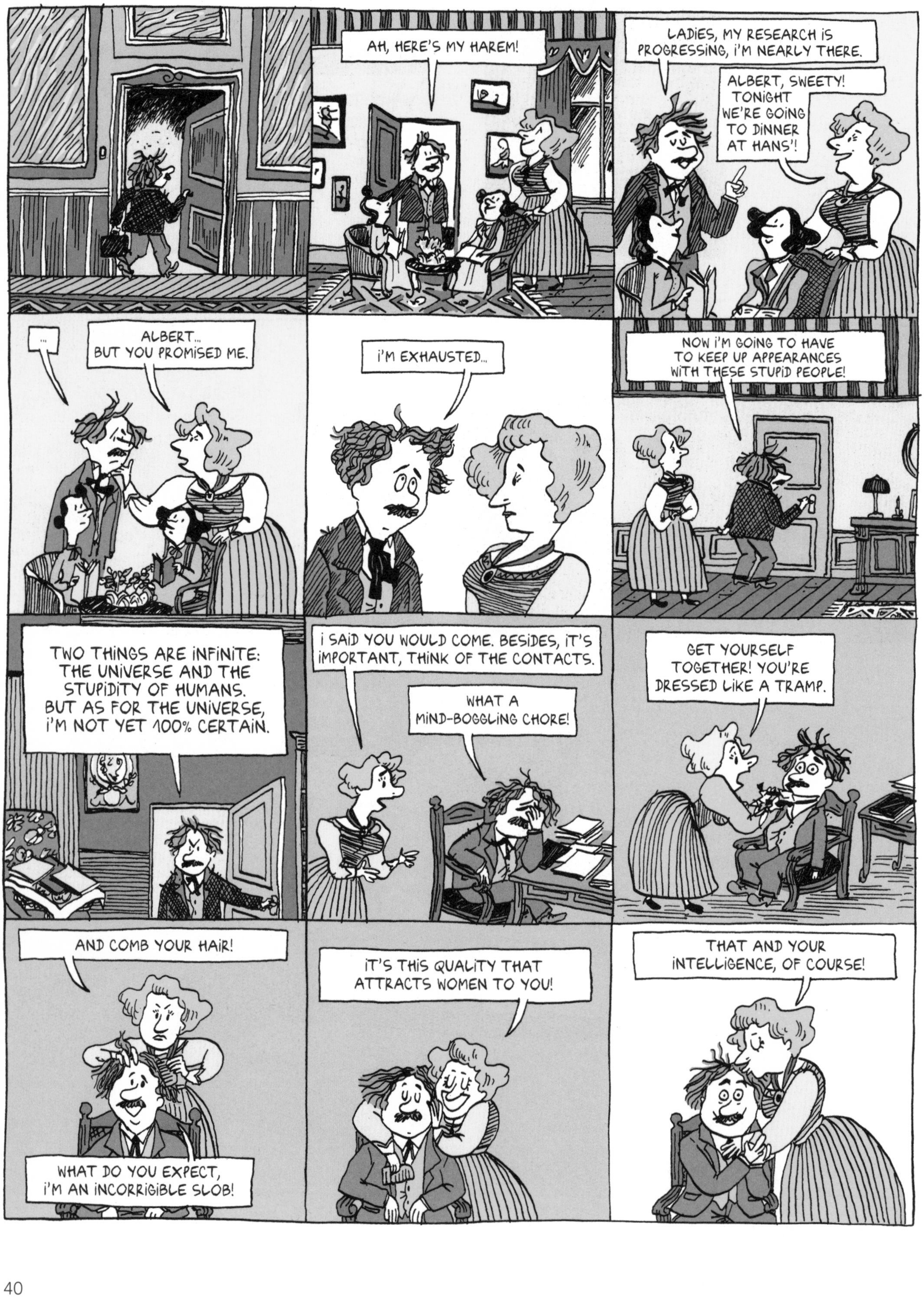
AH, HERE'S MY HAREM!
LADIES, MY RESEARCH IS PROGRESSING, I'M NEARLY THERE.
ALBERT, SWEETY! TONIGHT WE'RE GOING TO DINNER AT HANS'!
...
ALBERT... BUT YOU PROMISED ME.
I'M EXHAUSTED...
NOW I'M GOING TO HAVE TO KEEP UP APPEARANCES WITH THESE STUPID PEOPLE!
TWO THINGS ARE INFINITE: THE UNIVERSE AND THE STUPIDITY OF HUMANS. BUT AS FOR THE UNIVERSE, I'M NOT YET 100% CERTAIN.
I SAID YOU WOULD COME. BESIDES, IT'S IMPORTANT, THINK OF THE CONTACTS.
WHAT A MIND-BOGGLING CHORE!
GET YOURSELF TOGETHER! YOU'RE DRESSED LIKE A TRAMP.
AND COMB YOUR HAIR!
WHAT DO YOU EXPECT, I'M AN INCORRIGIBLE SLOB!
IT'S THIS QUALITY THAT ATTRACTS WOMEN TO YOU!
THAT AND YOUR INTELLIGENCE, OF COURSE!

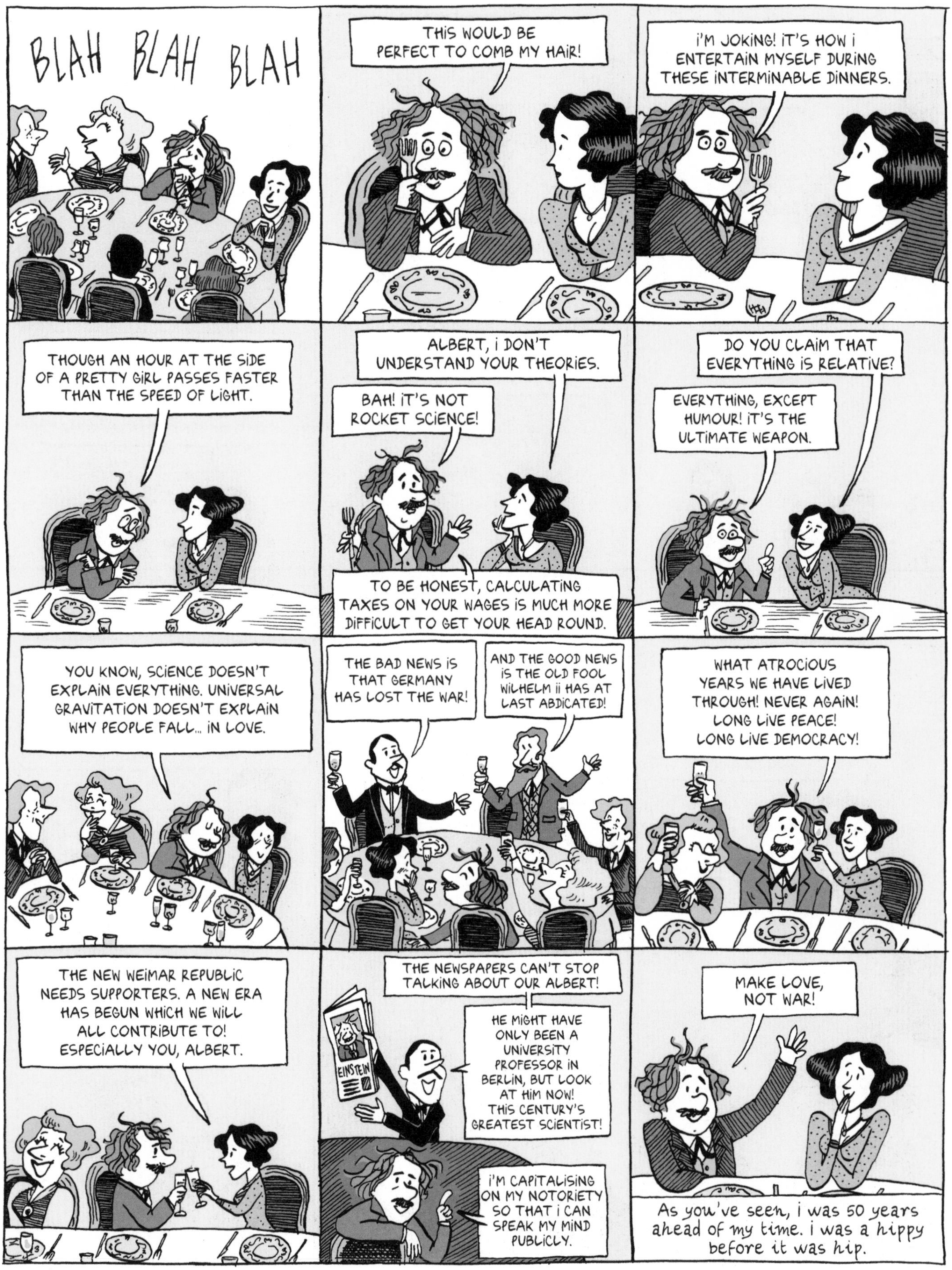
BLAH BLAH BLAH
THIS WOULD BE PERFECT TO COMB MY HAIR!
I'M JOKING! IT'S HOW I ENTERTAIN MYSELF DURING THESE INTERMINABLE DINNERS.
THOUGH AN HOUR AT THE SIDE OF A PRETTY GIRL PASSES FASTER THAN THE SPEED OF LIGHT.
ALBERT, I DON'T UNDERSTAND YOUR THEORIES.
BAH! IT'S NOT ROCKET SCIENCE!
TO BE HONEST, CALCULATING TAXES ON YOUR WAGES IS MUCH MORE DIFFICULT TO GET YOUR HEAD ROUND.
DO YOU CLAIM THAT EVERYTHING IS RELATIVE?
EVERYTHING, EXCEPT HUMOUR! IT'S THE ULTIMATE WEAPON.
YOU KNOW, SCIENCE DOESN'T EXPLAIN EVERYTHING. UNIVERSAL GRAVITATION DOESN'T EXPLAIN WHY PEOPLE FALL... IN LOVE.
THE BAD NEWS IS THAT GERMANY HAS LOST THE WAR!
AND THE GOOD NEWS IS THE OLD FOOL WILHELM II HAS AT LAST ABDICATED!
WHAT ATROCIOUS YEARS WE HAVE LIVED THROUGH! NEVER AGAIN! LONG LIVE PEACE! LONG LIVE DEMOCRACY!
THE NEW WEIMAR REPUBLIC NEEDS SUPPORTERS. A NEW ERA HAS BEGUN WHICH WE WILL ALL CONTRIBUTE TO! ESPECIALLY YOU, ALBERT.
THE NEWSPAPERS CAN'T STOP TALKING ABOUT OUR ALBERT!
EINSTEIN
HE MIGHT HAVE ONLY BEEN A UNIVERSITY PROFESSOR IN BERLIN, BUT LOOK AT HIM NOW! THIS CENTURY'S GREATEST SCIENTIST!
I'M CAPITALISING ON MY NOTORIETY SO THAT I CAN SPEAK MY MIND PUBLICLY.
MAKE LOVE, NOT WAR!
As you've seen, I was 50 years ahead of my time. I was a hippy before it was hip.

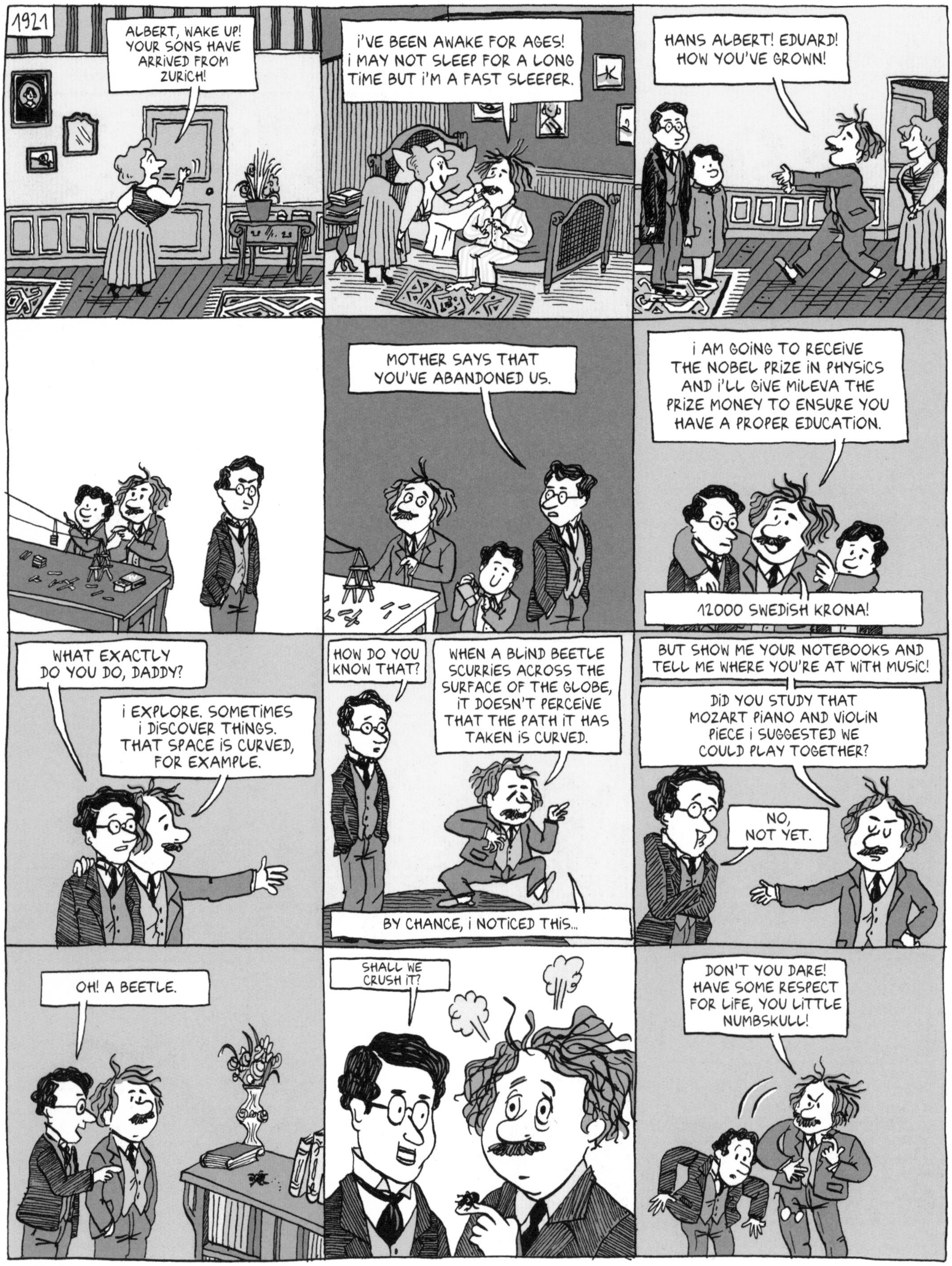
1921
ALBERT, WAKE UP! YOUR SONS HAVE ARRIVED FROM ZURICH!
I'VE BEEN AWAKE FOR AGES! I MAY NOT SLEEP FOR A LONG TIME BUT I'M A FAST SLEEPER.
HANS ALBERT! EDUARD! HOW YOU'VE GROWN!
MOTHER SAYS THAT YOU'VE ABANDONED US.
I AM GOING TO RECEIVE THE NOBEL PRIZE IN PHYSICS AND I'LL GIVE MILEVA THE PRIZE MONEY TO ENSURE YOU HAVE A PROPER EDUCATION.
12000 SWEDISH KRONA!
WHAT EXACTLY DO YOU DO, DADDY?
I EXPLORE. SOMETIMES I DISCOVER THINGS. THAT SPACE IS CURVED, FOR EXAMPLE.
HOW DO YOU KNOW THAT?
WHEN A BLIND BEETLE SCURRIES ACROSS THE SURFACE OF THE GLOBE, IT DOESN'T PERCEIVE THAT THE PATH IT HAS TAKEN IS CURVED.
BY CHANCE, I NOTICED THIS...
BUT SHOW ME YOUR NOTEBOOKS AND TELL ME WHERE YOU'RE AT WITH MUSIC!
DID YOU STUDY THAT MOZART PIANO AND VIOLIN PIECE I SUGGESTED WE COULD PLAY TOGETHER?
NO, NOT YET.
OH! A BEETLE.
SHALL WE CRUSH IT?
DON'T YOU DARE! HAVE SOME RESPECT FOR LIFE, YOU LITTLE NUMBSKULL!

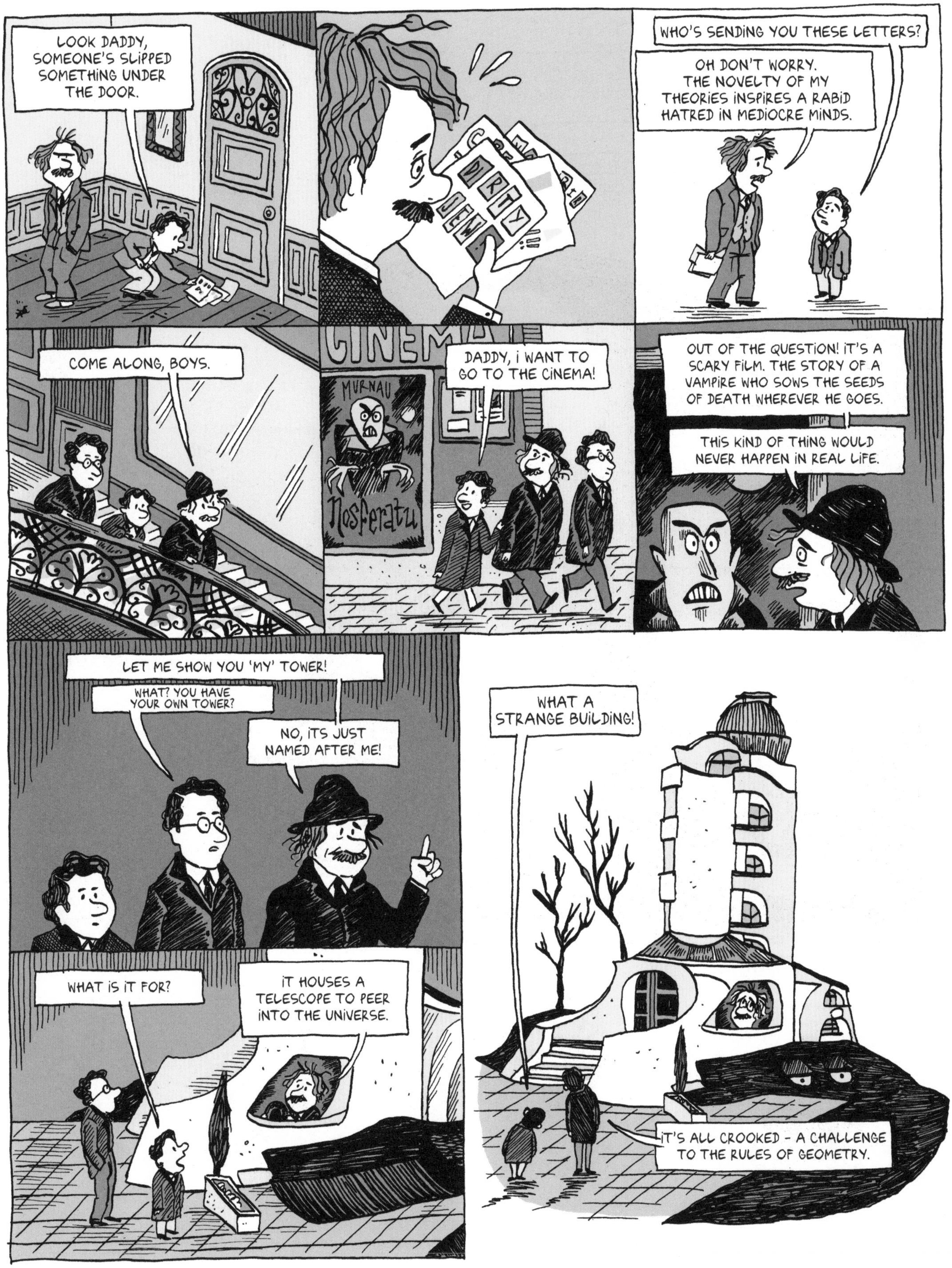
LOOK DADDY, SOMEONE'S SLIPPED SOMETHING UNDER THE DOOR.
DIRTY JEW
WHO'S SENDING YOU THESE LETTERS?
OH DON'T WORRY. THE NOVELTY OF MY THEORIES INSPIRES A RABID HATRED IN MEDIOCRE MINDS.
COME ALONG, BOYS.
CINEMA
MURNAU
Nosferatu
DADDY, I WANT TO GO TO THE CINEMA!
OUT OF THE QUESTION! IT'S A SCARY FILM. THE STORY OF A VAMPIRE WHO SOWS THE SEEDS OF DEATH WHEREVER HE GOES.
THIS KIND OF THING WOULD NEVER HAPPEN IN REAL LIFE.
LET ME SHOW YOU 'MY' TOWER!
WHAT? YOU HAVE YOUR OWN TOWER?
NO, ITS JUST NAMED AFTER ME!
WHAT IS IT FOR?
IT HOUSES A TELESCOPE TO PEER INTO THE UNIVERSE.
WHAT A STRANGE BUILDING!
IT'S ALL CROOKED - A CHALLENGE TO THE RULES OF GEOMETRY.

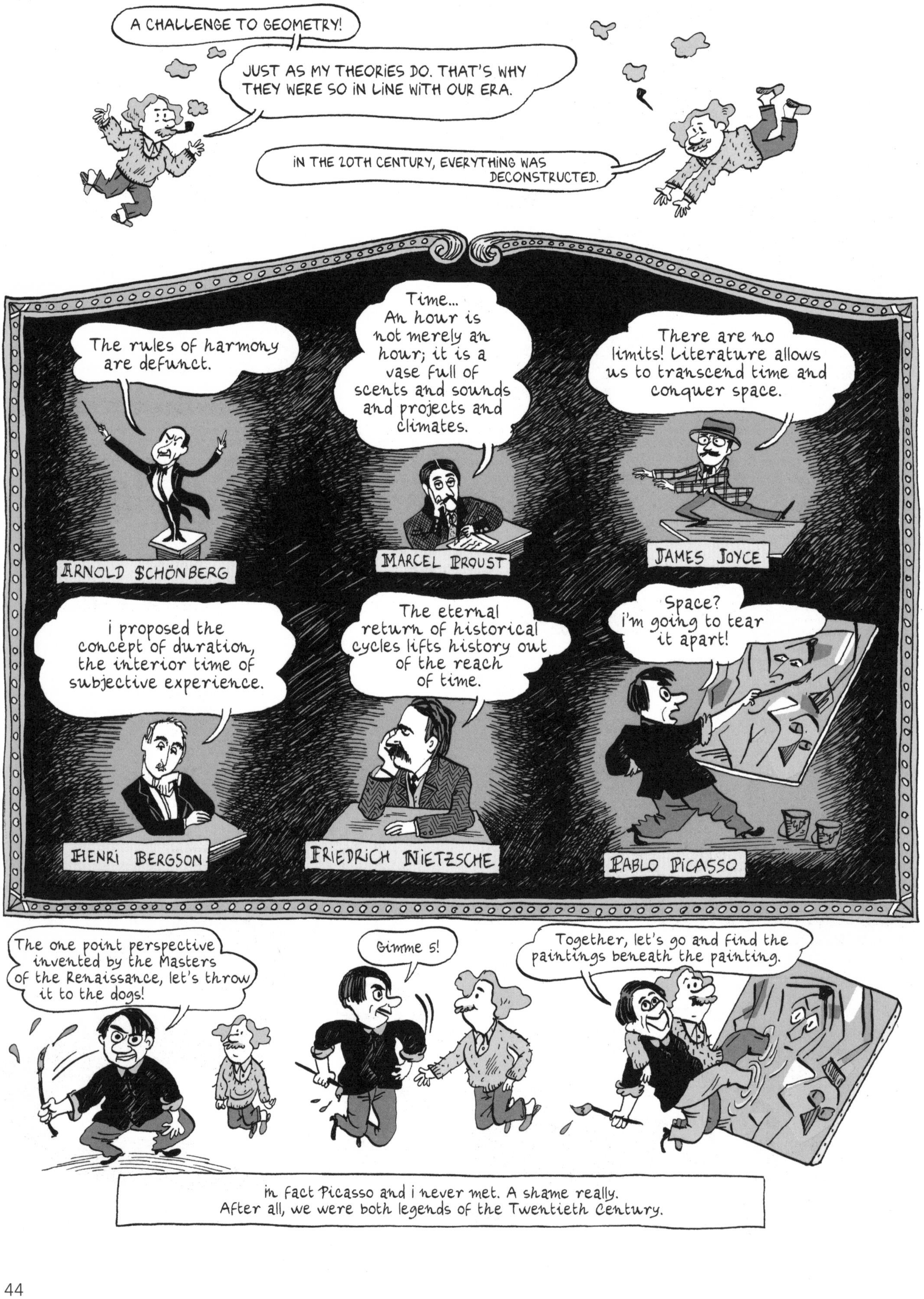
A CHALLENGE TO GEOMETRY!
JUST AS MY THEORIES DO. THAT'S WHY THEY WERE SO IN LINE WITH OUR ERA.
IN THE 20TH CENTURY, EVERYTHING WAS DECONSTRUCTED.
The rules of harmony are defunct.
ARNOLD SCHÖNBERG
Time... An hour is not merely an hour; it is a vase full of scents and sounds and projects and climates.
MARCEL PROUST
There are no limits! Literature allows us to transcend time and conquer space.
JAMES JOYCE
I proposed the concept of duration, the interior time of subjective experience.
HENRI BERGSON
The eternal return of historical cycles lifts history out of the reach of time.
FRIEDRICH NIETZSCHE
Space? I'm going to tear it apart!
PABLO PICASSO
The one point perspective invented by the Masters of the Renaissance, let's throw it to the dogs!
Gimme 5!
Together, let's go and find the paintings beneath the painting.
In fact Picasso and I never met. A shame really. After all, we were both legends of the Twentieth Century.

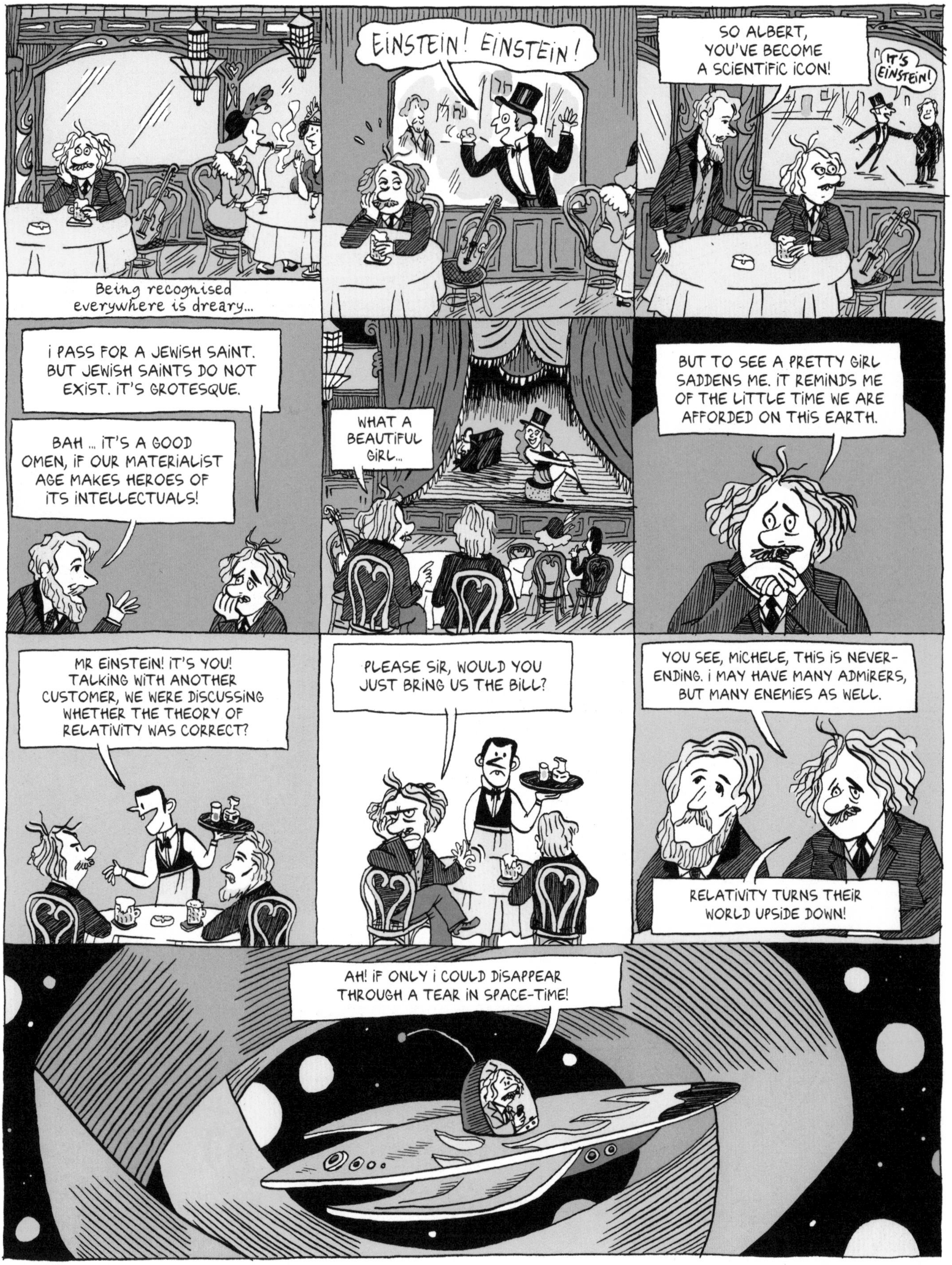
Being recognised everywhere is dreary...
EINSTEIN! EINSTEIN!
SO ALBERT, YOU'VE BECOME A SCIENTIFIC ICON!
IT'S EINSTEIN!
I PASS FOR A JEWISH SAINT. BUT JEWISH SAINTS DO NOT EXIST. IT'S GROTESQUE.
BAH ... IT'S A GOOD OMEN, IF OUR MATERIALIST AGE MAKES HEROES OF ITS INTELLECTUALS!
WHAT A BEAUTIFUL GIRL...
BUT TO SEE A PRETTY GIRL SADDENS ME. IT REMINDS ME OF THE LITTLE TIME WE ARE AFFORDED ON THIS EARTH.
MR EINSTEIN! IT'S YOU! TALKING WITH ANOTHER CUSTOMER, WE WERE DISCUSSING WHETHER THE THEORY OF RELATIVITY WAS CORRECT?
PLEASE SIR, WOULD YOU JUST BRING US THE BILL?
YOU SEE, MICHELE, THIS IS NEVER-ENDING. I MAY HAVE MANY ADMIRERS, BUT MANY ENEMIES AS WELL.
RELATIVITY TURNS THEIR WORLD UPSIDE DOWN!
AH! IF ONLY I COULD DISAPPEAR THROUGH A TEAR IN SPACE-TIME!

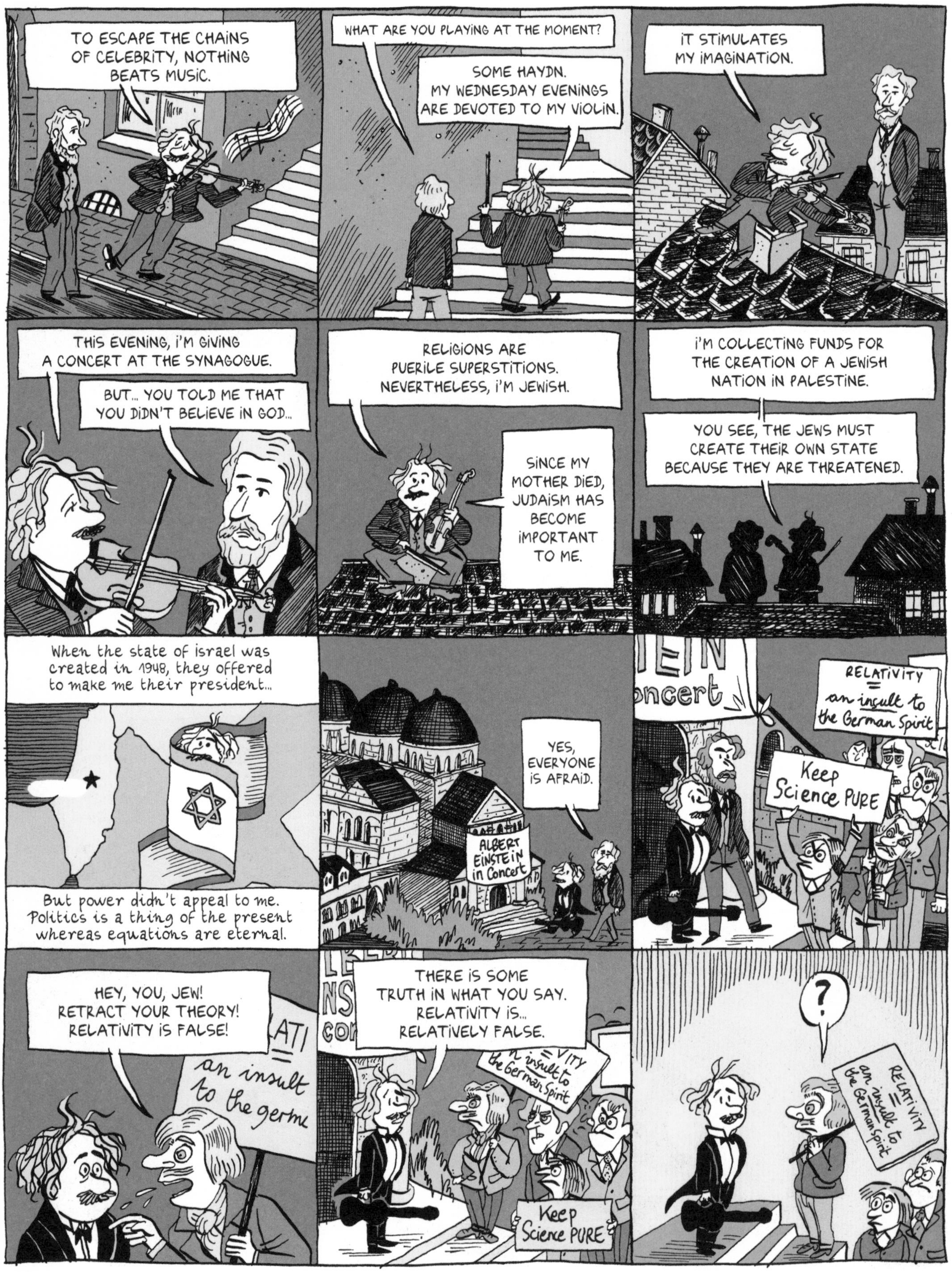
TO ESCAPE THE CHAINS OF CELEBRITY, NOTHING BEATS MUSIC.
WHAT ARE YOU PLAYING AT THE MOMENT?
SOME HAYDN. MY WEDNESDAY EVENINGS ARE DEVOTED TO MY VIOLIN.
IT STIMULATES MY IMAGINATION.
THIS EVENING, I'M GIVING A CONCERT AT THE SYNAGOGUE.
BUT... YOU TOLD ME THAT YOU DIDN'T BELIEVE IN GOD...
RELIGIONS ARE PUERILE SUPERSTITIONS. NEVERTHELESS, I'M JEWISH.
SINCE MY MOTHER DIED, JUDAISM HAS BECOME IMPORTANT TO ME.
I'M COLLECTING FUNDS FOR THE CREATION OF A JEWISH NATION IN PALESTINE.
YOU SEE, THE JEWS MUST CREATE THEIR OWN STATE BECAUSE THEY ARE THREATENED.
When the state of israel was created in 1948, they offered to make me their president...
But power didn't appeal to me. Politics is a thing of the present whereas equations are eternal.
ALBERT EINSTEIN in Concert
YES, EVERYONE IS AFRAID.
oncert
RELATIVITY = an insult to the German Spirit
Keep Science PURE
HEY, YOU, JEW! RETRACT YOUR THEORY! RELATIVITY IS FALSE!
an insult to the germ
THERE IS SOME TRUTH IN WHAT YOU SAY. RELATIVITY IS... RELATIVELY FALSE.
Keep Science PURE
?
RELATIVITY = an insult to the German Spirit

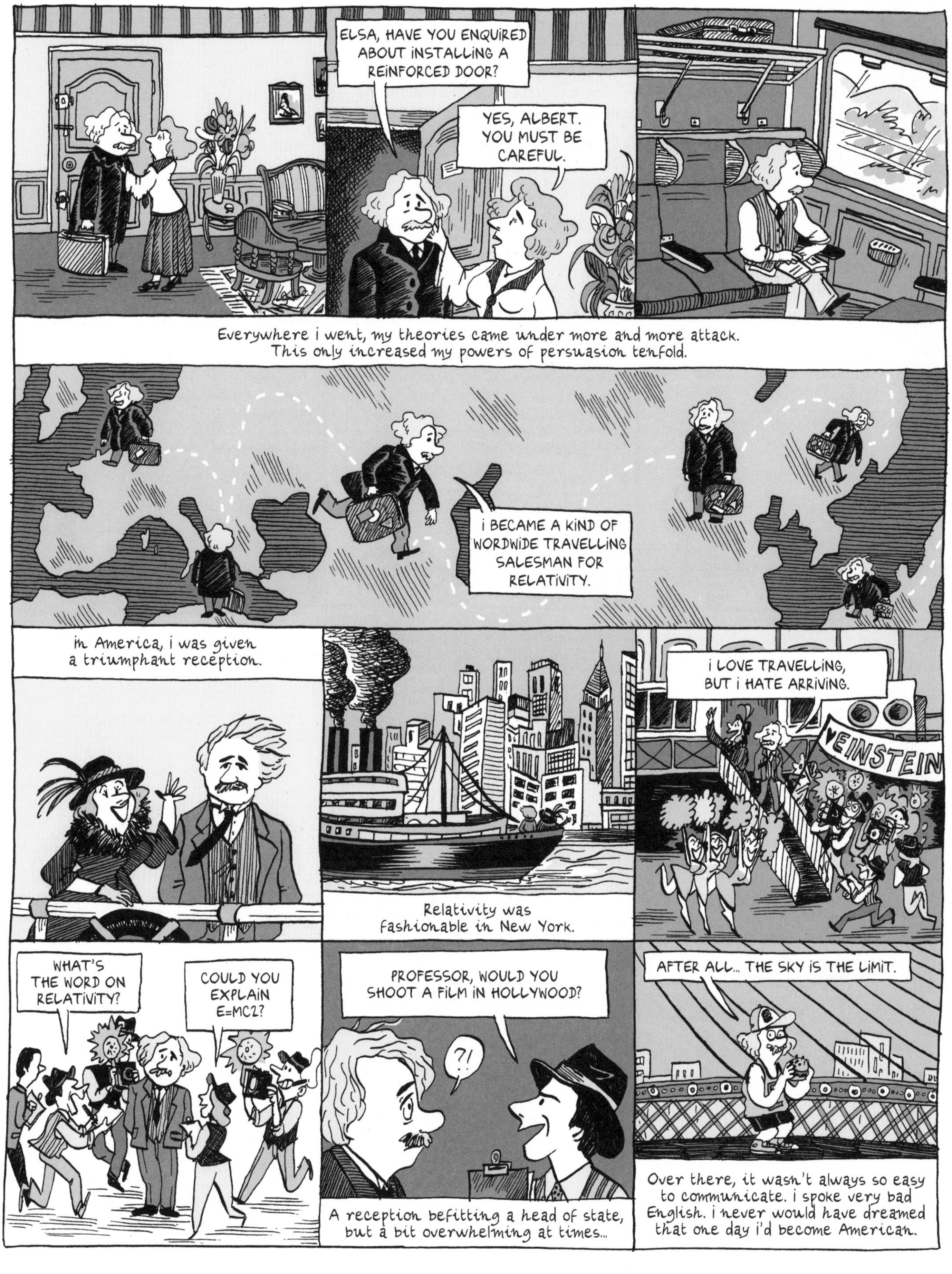
ELSA, HAVE YOU ENQUIRED ABOUT INSTALLING A REINFORCED DOOR?
YES, ALBERT. YOU MUST BE CAREFUL.
Everywhere i went, my theories came under more and more attack. This only increased my powers of persuasion tenfold.
i BECAME A KIND OF WORDWIDE TRAVELLING SALESMAN FOR RELATIVITY.
in America, i was given a triumphant reception.
Relativity was fashionable in New York.
i LOVE TRAVELLING, BUT i HATE ARRIVING.
♥EINSTEIN
WHAT'S THE WORD ON RELATIVITY?
COULD YOU EXPLAIN E=MC2?
PROFESSOR, WOULD YOU SHOOT A FILM IN HOLLYWOOD?
?!
A reception befitting a head of state, but a bit overwhelming at times...
AFTER ALL... THE SKY IS THE LIMIT.
Over there, it wasn't always so easy to communicate. i spoke very bad English. i never would have dreamed that one day i'd become American.

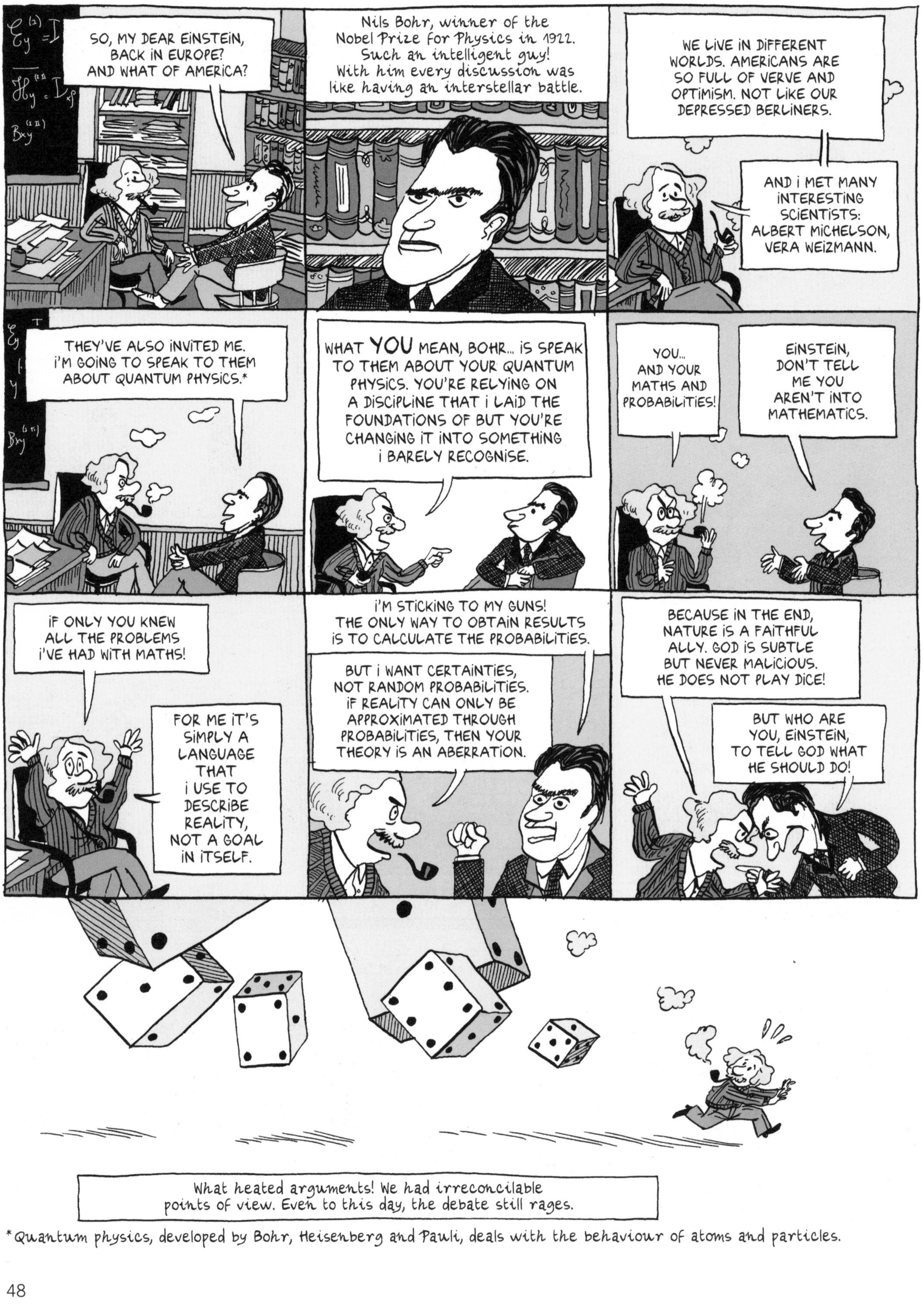
SO, MY DEAR EINSTEIN, BACK IN EUROPE? AND WHAT OF AMERICA?
Nils Bohr, winner of the Nobel Prize for Physics in 1922. Such an intelligent guy! With him every discussion was like having an interstellar battle.
WE LIVE IN DIFFERENT WORLDS. AMERICANS ARE SO FULL OF VERVE AND OPTIMISM. NOT LIKE OUR DEPRESSED BERLINERS.
AND I MET MANY INTERESTING SCIENTISTS: ALBERT MICHELSON, VERA WEIZMANN.
THEY'VE ALSO INVITED ME. I'M GOING TO SPEAK TO THEM ABOUT QUANTUM PHYSICS.*
WHAT YOU MEAN, BOHR... IS SPEAK TO THEM ABOUT YOUR QUANTUM PHYSICS. YOU'RE RELYING ON A DISCIPLINE THAT I LAID THE FOUNDATIONS OF BUT YOU'RE CHANGING IT INTO SOMETHING I BARELY RECOGNISE.
YOU... AND YOUR MATHS AND PROBABILITIES!
EINSTEIN, DON'T TELL ME YOU AREN'T INTO MATHEMATICS.
IF ONLY YOU KNEW ALL THE PROBLEMS I'VE HAD WITH MATHS!
FOR ME IT'S SIMPLY A LANGUAGE THAT I USE TO DESCRIBE REALITY, NOT A GOAL IN ITSELF.
I'M STICKING TO MY GUNS! THE ONLY WAY TO OBTAIN RESULTS IS TO CALCULATE THE PROBABILITIES.
BUT I WANT CERTAINTIES, NOT RANDOM PROBABILITIES. IF REALITY CAN ONLY BE APPROXIMATED THROUGH PROBABILITIES, THEN YOUR THEORY IS AN ABERRATION.
BECAUSE IN THE END, NATURE IS A FAITHFUL ALLY. GOD IS SUBTLE BUT NEVER MALICIOUS. HE DOES NOT PLAY DICE!
BUT WHO ARE YOU, EINSTEIN, TO TELL GOD WHAT HE SHOULD DO!
What heated arguments! We had irreconcilable points of view. Even to this day, the debate still rages.

*Quantum physics, developed by Bohr, Heisenberg and Pauli, deals with the behaviour of atoms and particles.

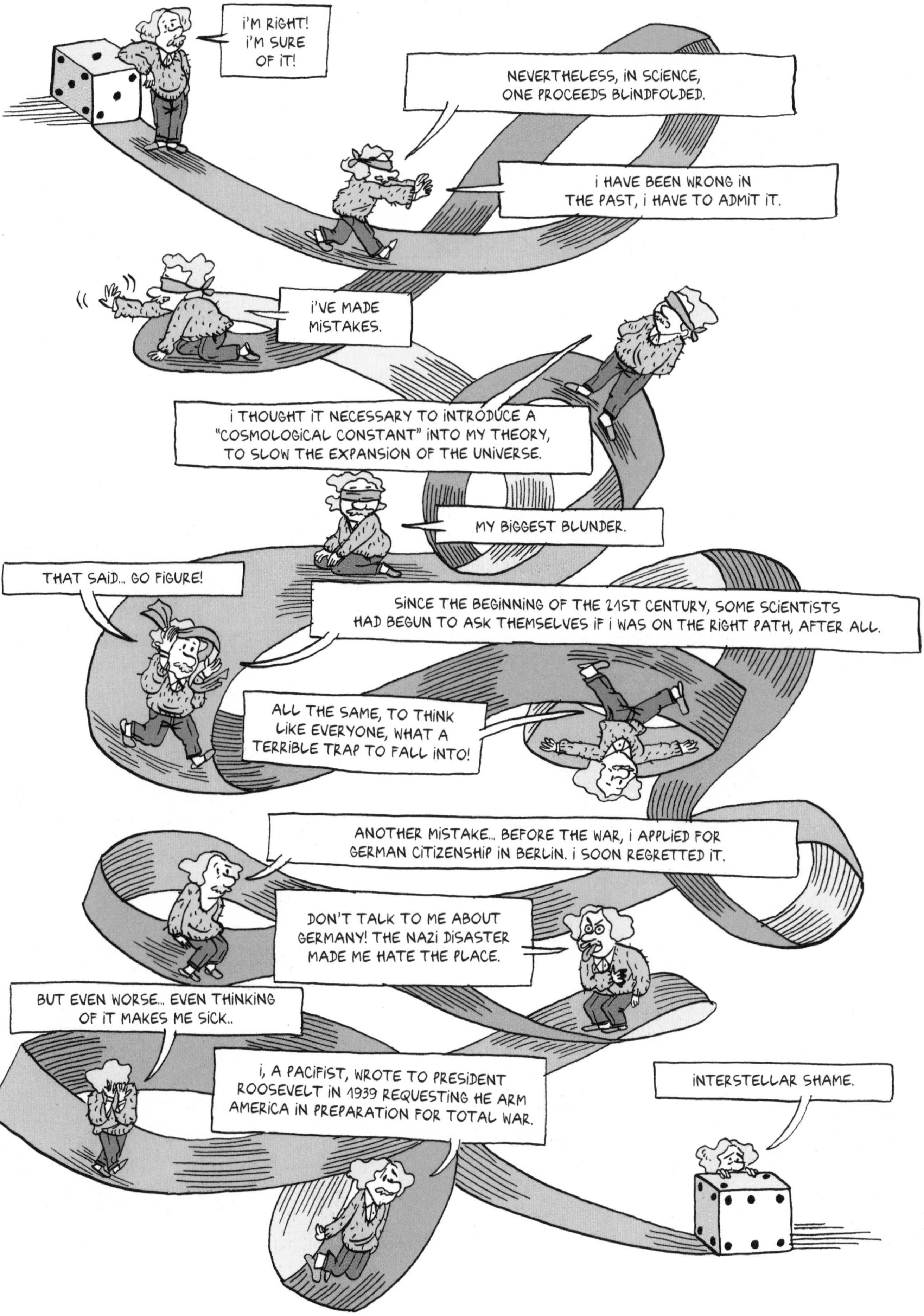
I'M RIGHT! I'M SURE OF IT!
NEVERTHELESS, IN SCIENCE, ONE PROCEEDS BLINDFOLDED.
I HAVE BEEN WRONG IN THE PAST, I HAVE TO ADMIT IT.
I'VE MADE MISTAKES.
I THOUGHT IT NECESSARY TO INTRODUCE A "COSMOLOGICAL CONSTANT" INTO MY THEORY, TO SLOW THE EXPANSION OF THE UNIVERSE.
MY BIGGEST BLUNDER.
THAT SAID... GO FIGURE!
SINCE THE BEGINNING OF THE 21ST CENTURY, SOME SCIENTISTS HAD BEGUN TO ASK THEMSELVES IF I WAS ON THE RIGHT PATH, AFTER ALL.
ALL THE SAME, TO THINK LIKE EVERYONE, WHAT A TERRIBLE TRAP TO FALL INTO!
ANOTHER MISTAKE... BEFORE THE WAR, I APPLIED FOR GERMAN CITIZENSHIP IN BERLIN. I SOON REGRETTED IT.
DON'T TALK TO ME ABOUT GERMANY! THE NAZI DISASTER MADE ME HATE THE PLACE.
BUT EVEN WORSE... EVEN THINKING OF IT MAKES ME SICK..
I, A PACIFIST, WROTE TO PRESIDENT ROOSEVELT IN 1939 REQUESTING HE ARM AMERICA IN PREPARATION FOR TOTAL WAR.
INTERSTELLAR SHAME.

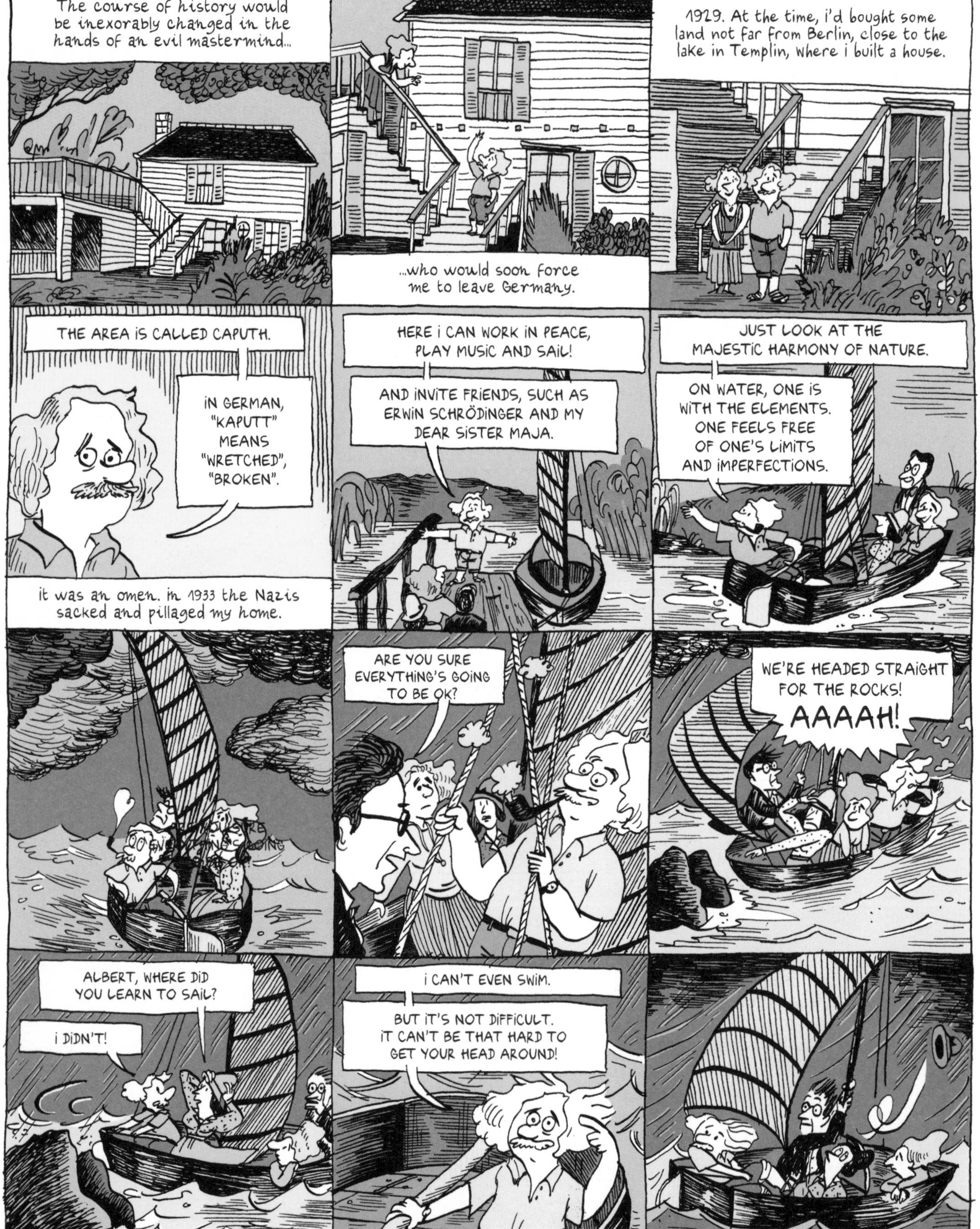
The course of history would be inexorably changed in the hands of an evil mastermind...
...who would soon force me to leave Germany.
1929. At the time, i'd bought some land not far from Berlin, close to the lake in Templin, where i built a house.
THE AREA iS CALLED CAPUTH.
iN GERMAN, "KAPUTT" MEANS "WRETCHED", "BROKEN".
it was an omen. in 1933 the Nazis sacked and pillaged my home.
HERE i CAN WORK iN PEACE, PLAY MUSiC AND SAiL!
AND iNViTE FRiENDS, SUCH AS ERWiN SCHRÖDiNGER AND MY DEAR SiSTER MAJA.
JUST LOOK AT THE MAJESTiC HARMONY OF NATURE.
ON WATER, ONE iS WiTH THE ELEMENTS. ONE FEELS FREE OF ONE'S LiMiTS AND iMPERFECTiONS.
ARE YOU SURE EVERYTHiNG'S GOiNG TO BE OK?
WE'RE HEADED STRAiGHT FOR THE ROCKS!
AAAAH!
ALBERT, WHERE DiD YOU LEARN TO SAiL?
i DiDN'T!
i CAN'T EVEN SWiM.
BUT iT'S NOT DiFFiCULT. iT CAN'T BE THAT HARD TO GET YOUR HEAD AROUND!

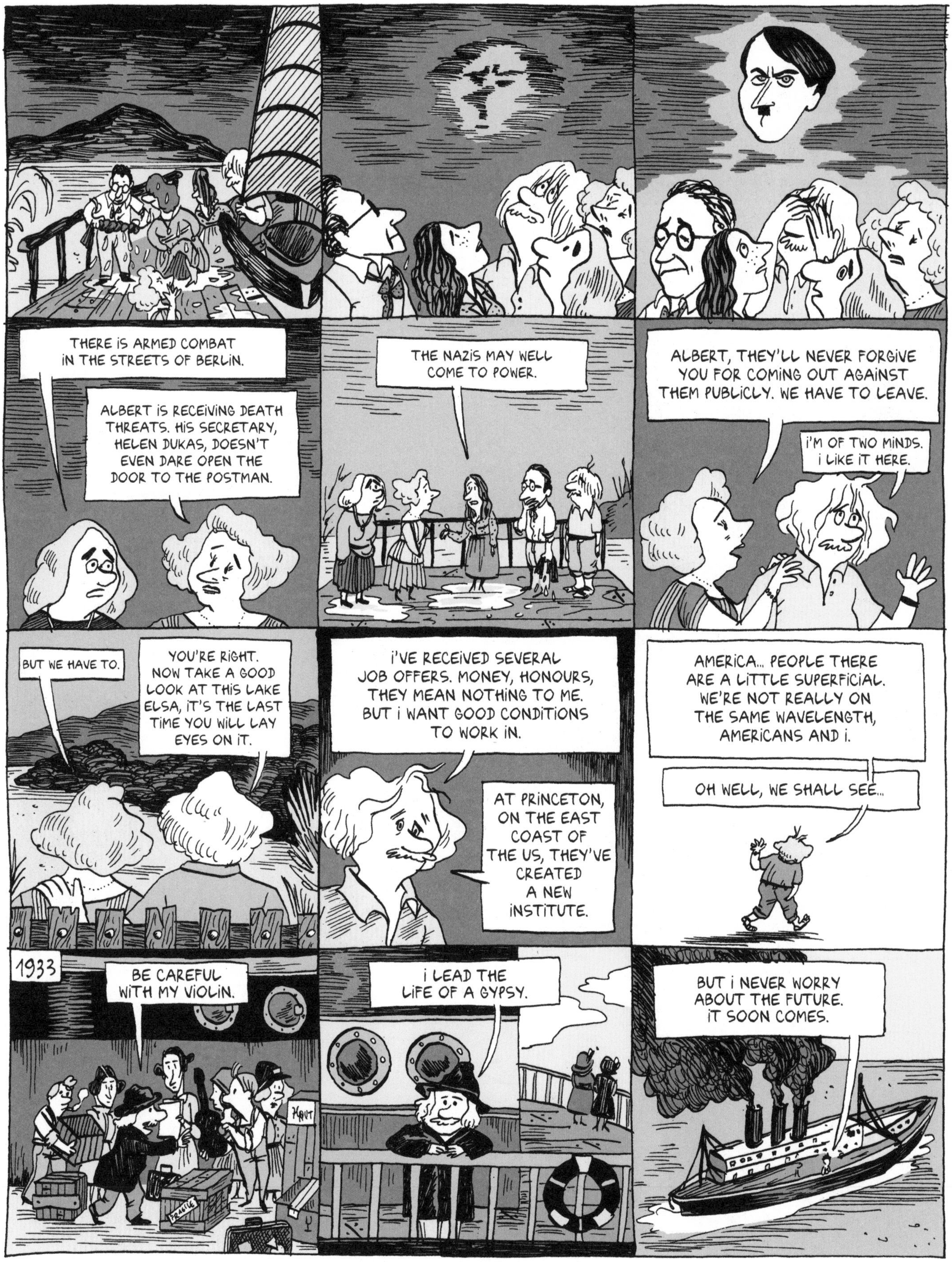
THERE IS ARMED COMBAT IN THE STREETS OF BERLIN.
ALBERT IS RECEIVING DEATH THREATS. HIS SECRETARY, HELEN DUKAS, DOESN'T EVEN DARE OPEN THE DOOR TO THE POSTMAN.
THE NAZIS MAY WELL COME TO POWER.
ALBERT, THEY'LL NEVER FORGIVE YOU FOR COMING OUT AGAINST THEM PUBLICLY. WE HAVE TO LEAVE.
I'M OF TWO MINDS. I LIKE IT HERE.
BUT WE HAVE TO.
YOU'RE RIGHT. NOW TAKE A GOOD LOOK AT THIS LAKE ELSA, IT'S THE LAST TIME YOU WILL LAY EYES ON IT.
I'VE RECEIVED SEVERAL JOB OFFERS. MONEY, HONOURS, THEY MEAN NOTHING TO ME. BUT I WANT GOOD CONDITIONS TO WORK IN.
AT PRINCETON, ON THE EAST COAST OF THE US, THEY'VE CREATED A NEW INSTITUTE.
AMERICA... PEOPLE THERE ARE A LITTLE SUPERFICIAL. WE'RE NOT REALLY ON THE SAME WAVELENGTH, AMERICANS AND I.
OH WELL, WE SHALL SEE...
1933
BE CAREFUL WITH MY VIOLIN.
I LEAD THE LIFE OF A GYPSY.
BUT I NEVER WORRY ABOUT THE FUTURE. IT SOON COMES.

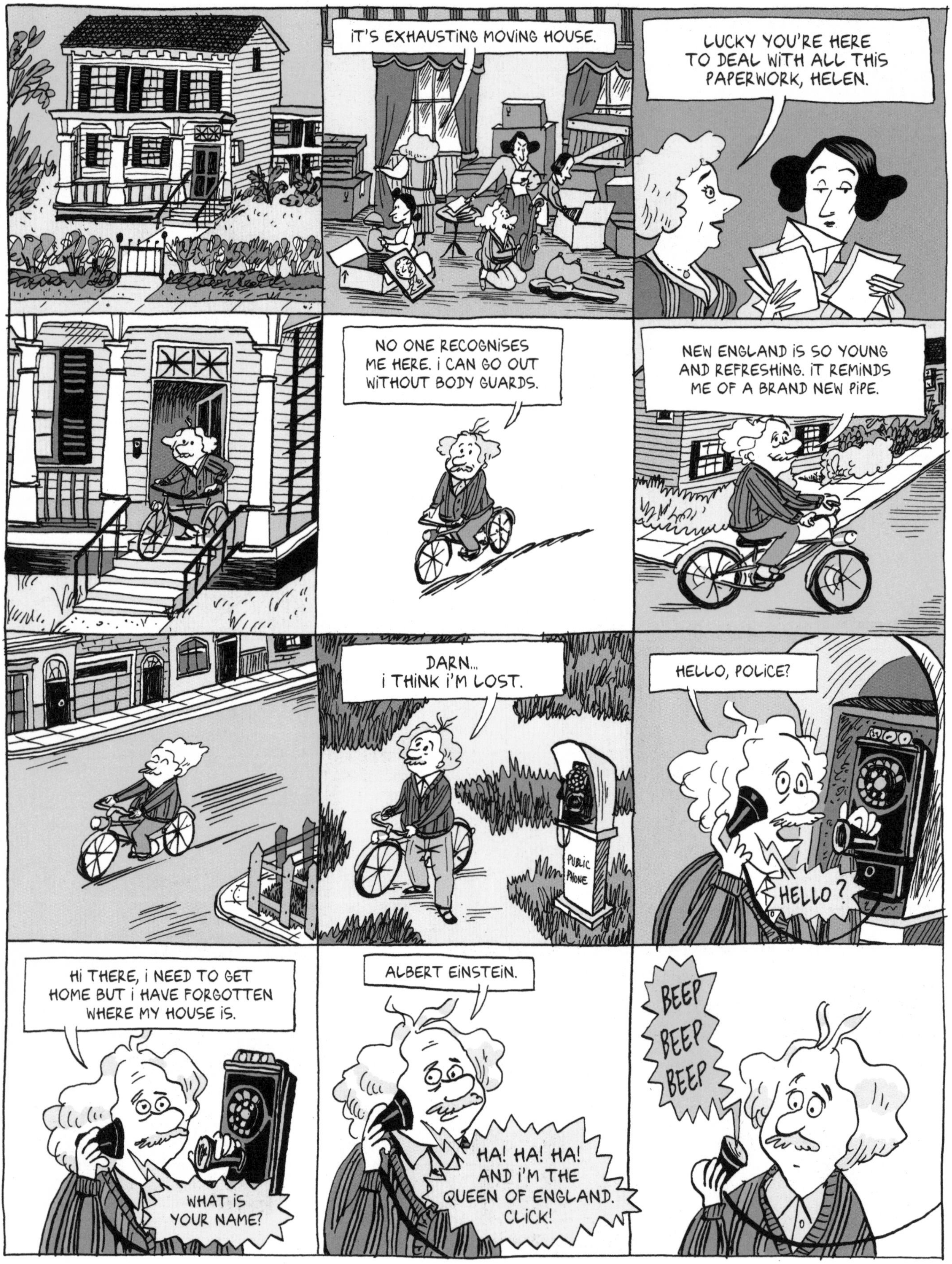

IT'S EXHAUSTING MOVING HOUSE.
LUCKY YOU'RE HERE TO DEAL WITH ALL THIS PAPERWORK, HELEN.
NO ONE RECOGNISES ME HERE. I CAN GO OUT WITHOUT BODY GUARDS.
NEW ENGLAND IS SO YOUNG AND REFRESHING. IT REMINDS ME OF A BRAND NEW PIPE.
DARN... I THINK I'M LOST.
PUBLIC PHONE
HELLO, POLICE?
HELLO ?
HI THERE, I NEED TO GET HOME BUT I HAVE FORGOTTEN WHERE MY HOUSE IS.
WHAT IS YOUR NAME?
ALBERT EINSTEIN.
HA! HA! HA! AND I'M THE QUEEN OF ENGLAND. CLICK!
BEEP BEEP BEEP

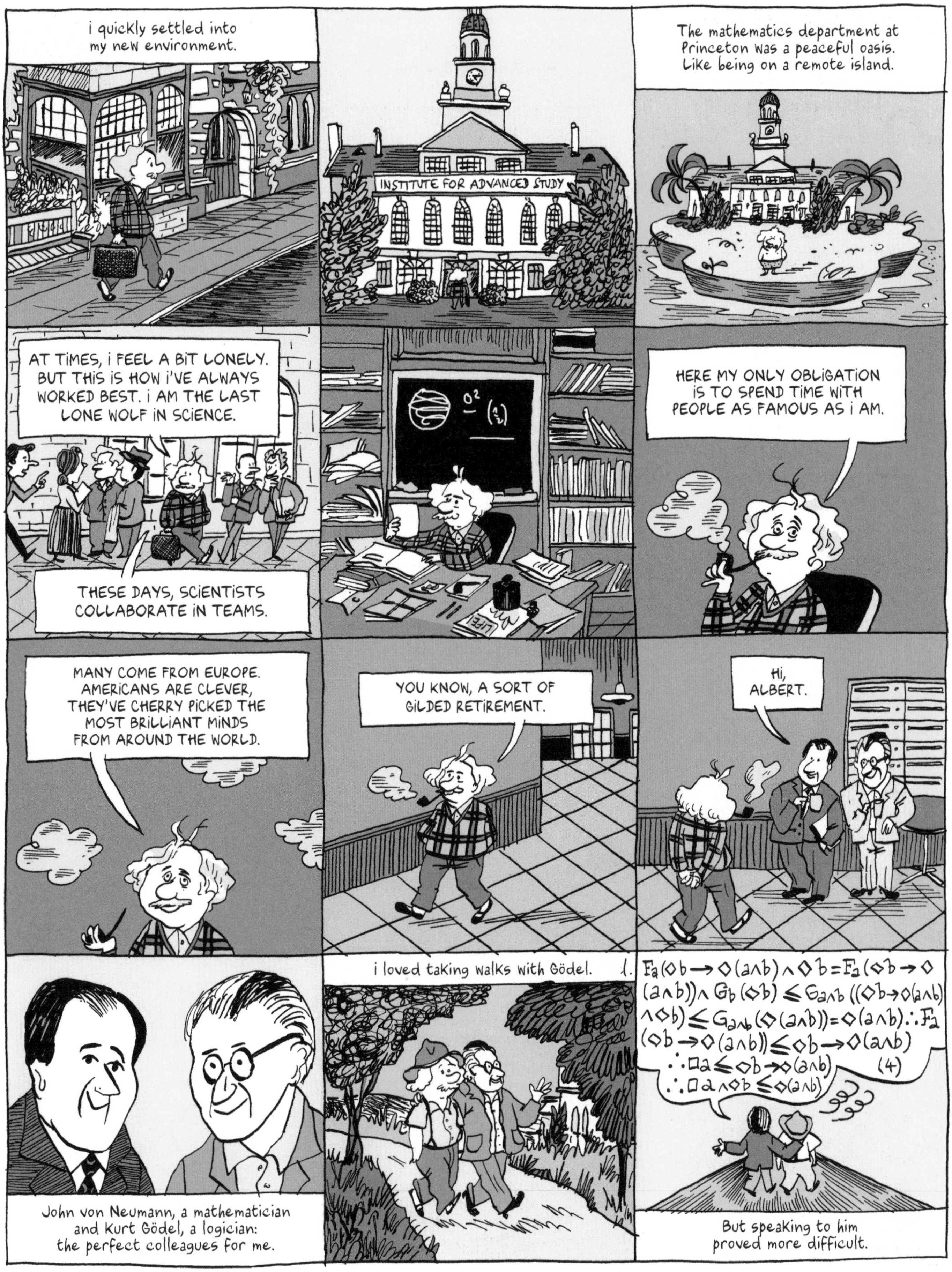
i quickly settled into my new environment.
INSTITUTE FOR ADVANCED STUDY
The mathematics department at Princeton was a peaceful oasis. Like being on a remote island.
AT TIMES, i FEEL A BIT LONELY. BUT THIS IS HOW i'VE ALWAYS WORKED BEST. i AM THE LAST LONE WOLF IN SCIENCE.
THESE DAYS, SCIENTISTS COLLABORATE IN TEAMS.
LIFE
HERE MY ONLY OBLIGATION IS TO SPEND TIME WITH PEOPLE AS FAMOUS AS i AM.
MANY COME FROM EUROPE. AMERICANS ARE CLEVER, THEY'VE CHERRY PICKED THE MOST BRILLIANT MINDS FROM AROUND THE WORLD.
YOU KNOW, A SORT OF GILDED RETIREMENT.
Hi, ALBERT.
John von Neumann, a mathematician and Kurt Gödel, a logician: the perfect colleagues for me.
i loved taking walks with Gödel.
1. Fa(◇b → ◇(a∧b) ∧ ◇b = Fa(◇b → ◇(a∧b)) ∧ Gb(◇b) ≤ Ga∧b ((◇b→◇(a∧b) ∧◇b) ≤ Ga∧b(◇(a∧b)) = ◇(a∧b) ∴ Fa (◇b → ◇(a∧b)) ≤ ◇b → ◇(a∧b)
∴ □a ≤ ◇b → ◇(a∧b) (4)
∴ □a ∧ ◇b ≤ ◇(a∧b)
But speaking to him proved more difficult.

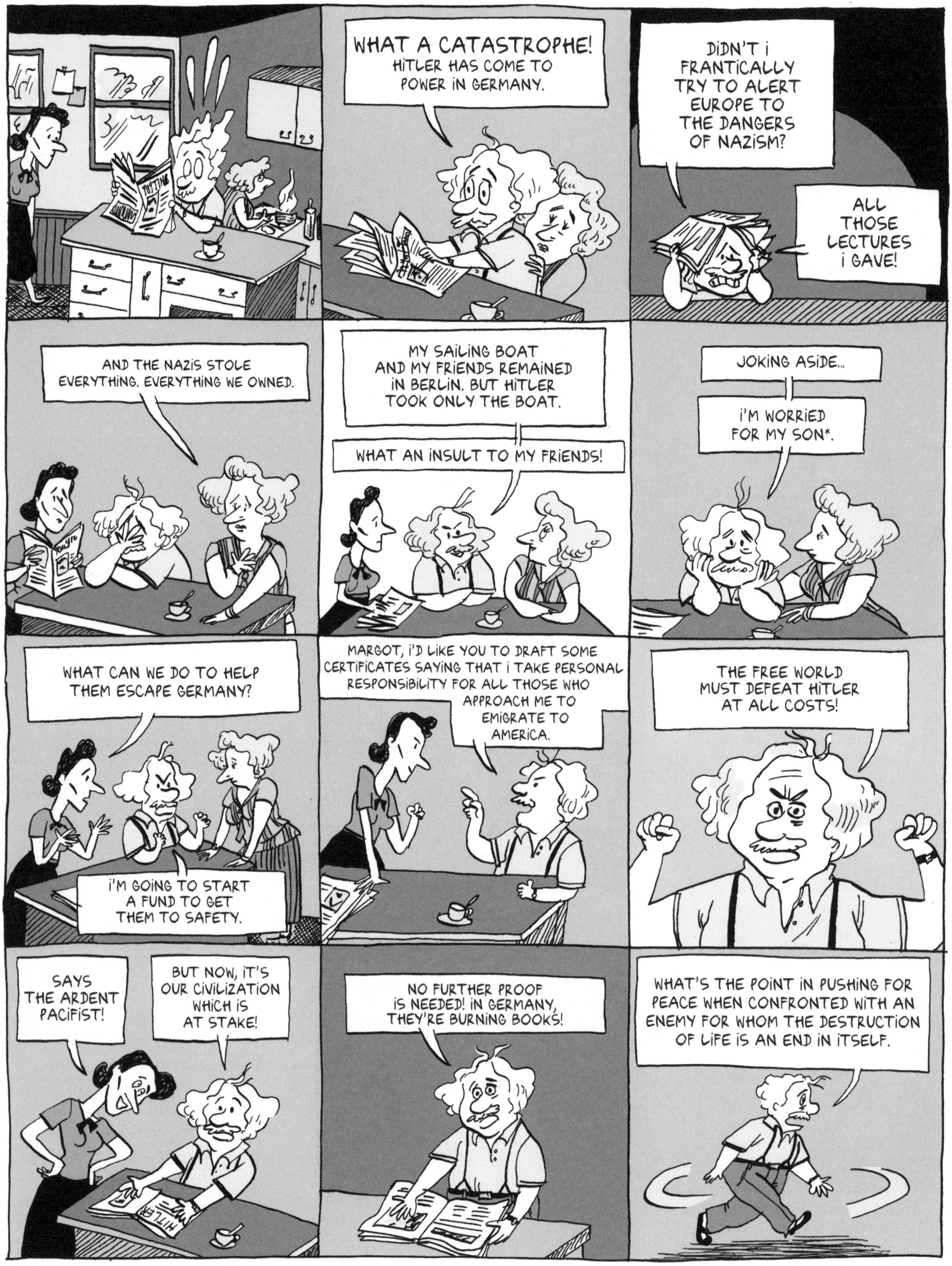

WHAT A CATASTROPHE! HITLER HAS COME TO POWER IN GERMANY.
DIDN'T I FRANTICALLY TRY TO ALERT EUROPE TO THE DANGERS OF NAZISM?
ALL THOSE LECTURES I GAVE!
AND THE NAZIS STOLE EVERYTHING. EVERYTHING WE OWNED.
MY SAILING BOAT AND MY FRIENDS REMAINED IN BERLIN. BUT HITLER TOOK ONLY THE BOAT.
WHAT AN INSULT TO MY FRIENDS!
JOKING ASIDE...
I'M WORRIED FOR MY SON*.
WHAT CAN WE DO TO HELP THEM ESCAPE GERMANY?
I'M GOING TO START A FUND TO GET THEM TO SAFETY.
MARGOT, I'D LIKE YOU TO DRAFT SOME CERTIFICATES SAYING THAT I TAKE PERSONAL RESPONSIBILITY FOR ALL THOSE WHO APPROACH ME TO EMIGRATE TO AMERICA.
THE FREE WORLD MUST DEFEAT HITLER AT ALL COSTS!
SAYS THE ARDENT PACIFIST!
BUT NOW, IT'S OUR CIVILIZATION WHICH IS AT STAKE!
NO FURTHER PROOF IS NEEDED! IN GERMANY, THEY'RE BURNING BOOKS!
WHAT'S THE POINT IN PUSHING FOR PEACE WHEN CONFRONTED WITH AN ENEMY FOR WHOM THE DESTRUCTION OF LIFE IS AN END IN ITSELF.

* Hans Albert emigrated to the United States in 1938. He became a professor of hydraulic engineering in Berkeley, California. Mileva and Eduard stayed in Switzerland, safe from harm.

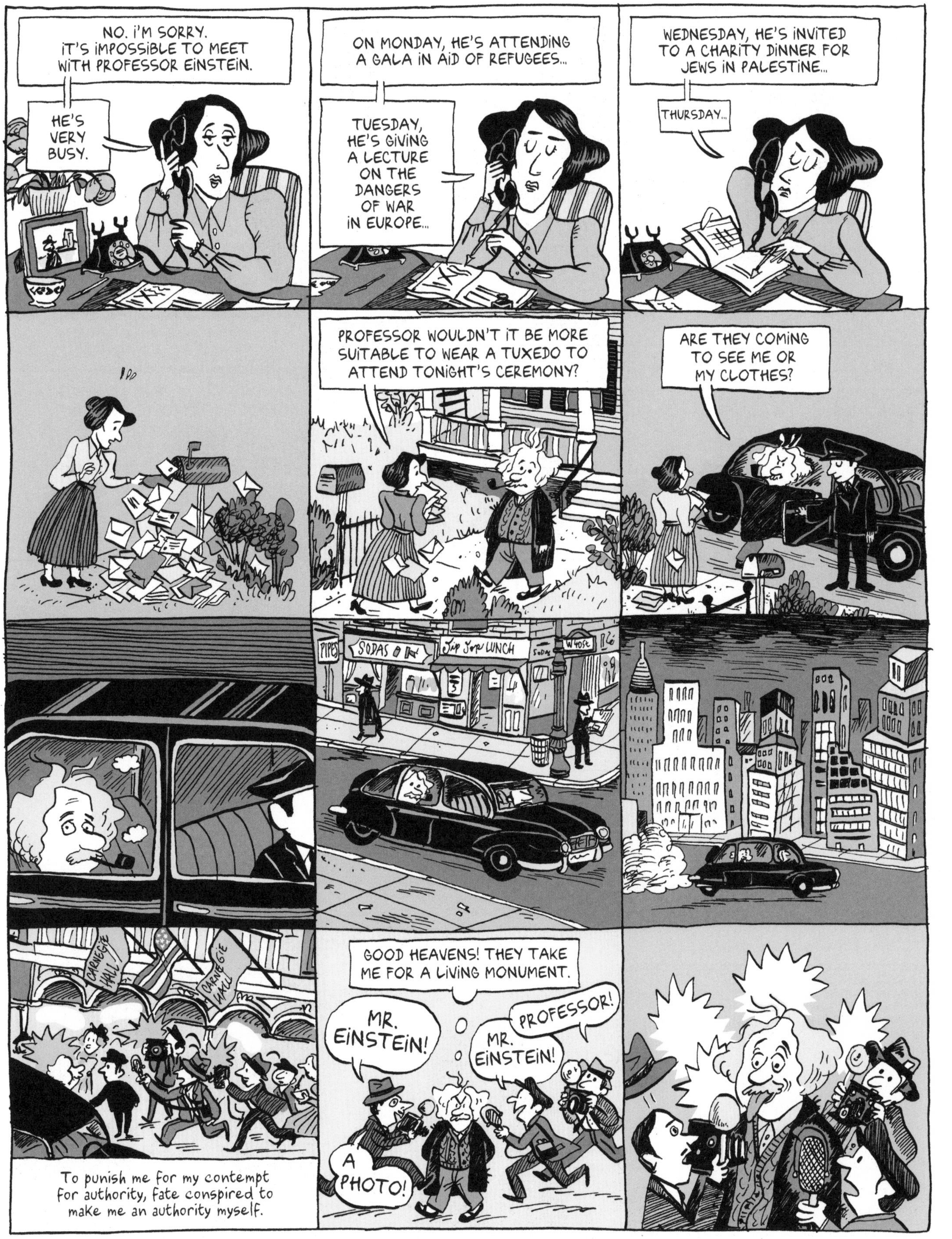
NO. I'M SORRY. IT'S IMPOSSIBLE TO MEET WITH PROFESSOR EINSTEIN.
HE'S VERY BUSY.
ON MONDAY, HE'S ATTENDING A GALA IN AID OF REFUGEES...
TUESDAY, HE'S GIVING A LECTURE ON THE DANGERS OF WAR IN EUROPE...
WEDNESDAY, HE'S INVITED TO A CHARITY DINNER FOR JEWS IN PALESTINE...
THURSDAY...
PROFESSOR WOULDN'T IT BE MORE SUITABLE TO WEAR A TUXEDO TO ATTEND TONIGHT'S CEREMONY?
ARE THEY COMING TO SEE ME OR MY CLOTHES?
PIPES
SODAS
LUNCH
CARNEGIE HALL
CARNEGIE HALL
To punish me for my contempt for authority, fate conspired to make me an authority myself.
GOOD HEAVENS! THEY TAKE ME FOR A LIVING MONUMENT.
MR. EINSTEIN!
MR. EINSTEIN!
PROFESSOR!
A PHOTO!

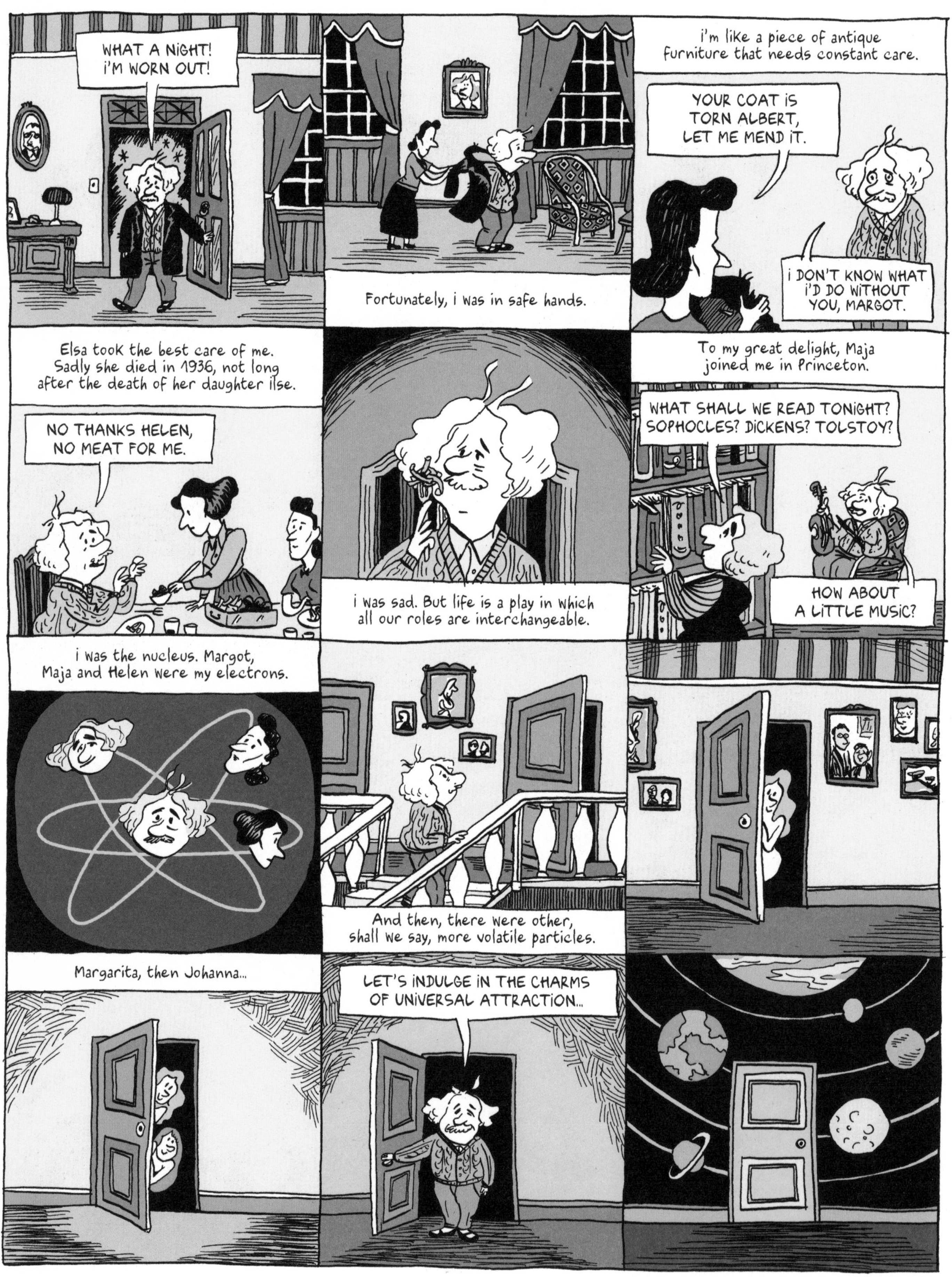
WHAT A NIGHT!
i'M WORN OUT!
Fortunately, i was in safe hands.
i'm like a piece of antique furniture that needs constant care.
YOUR COAT iS TORN ALBERT, LET ME MEND iT.
i DON'T KNOW WHAT i'D DO WiTHOUT YOU, MARGOT.
Elsa took the best care of me. Sadly she died in 1936, not long after the death of her daughter ilse.
NO THANKS HELEN, NO MEAT FOR ME.
i was sad. But life is a play in which all our roles are interchangeable.
To my great delight, Maja joined me in Princeton.
WHAT SHALL WE READ TONiGHT? SOPHOCLES? DiCKENS? TOLSTOY?
HOW ABOUT A LiTTLE MUSiC?
i was the nucleus. Margot, Maja and Helen were my electrons.
And then, there were other, shall we say, more volatile particles.
Margarita, then Johanna...
LET'S iNDULGE iN THE CHARMS OF UNiVERSAL ATTRACTiON...

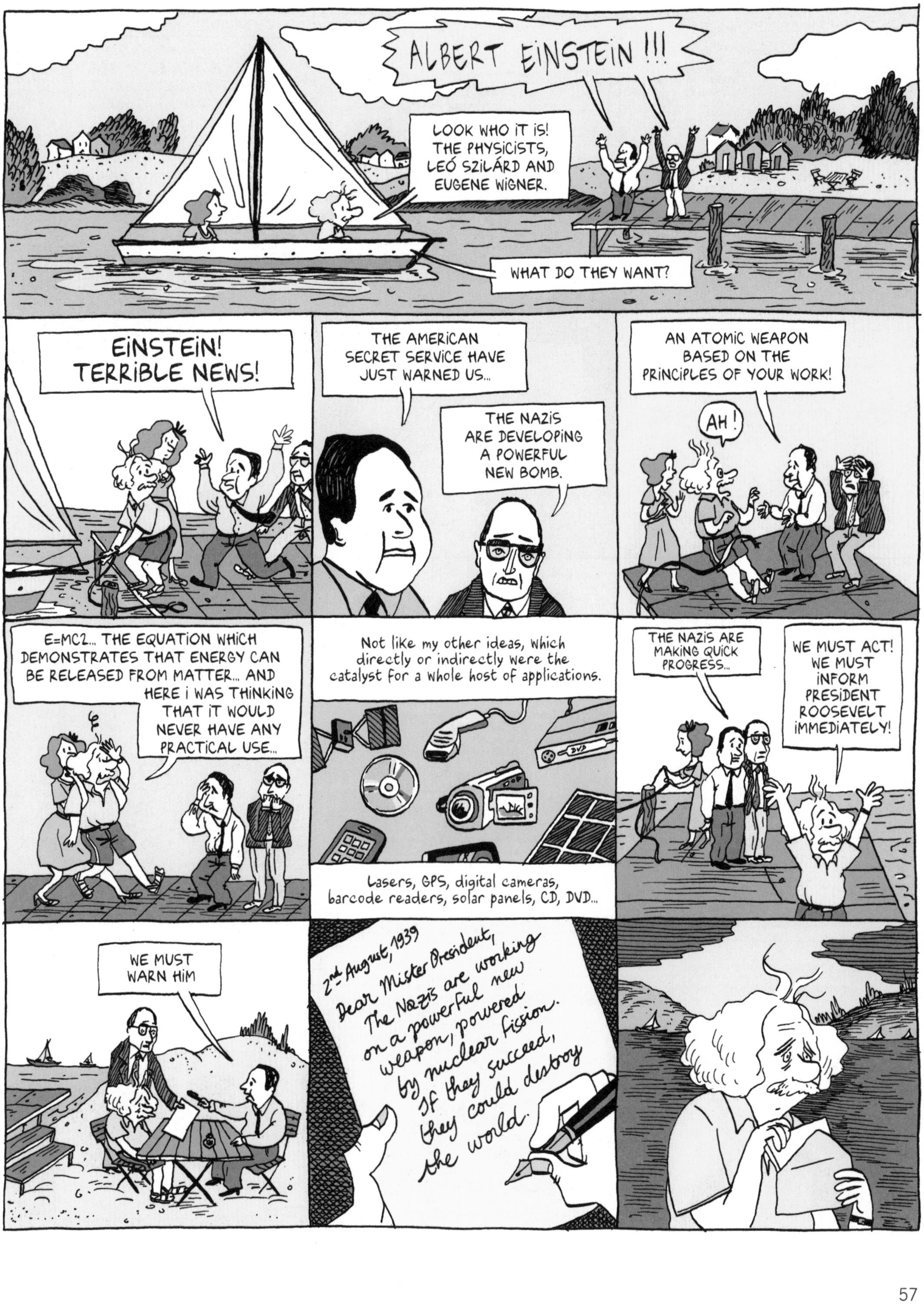
ALBERT EINSTEIN !!!
LOOK WHO IT IS! THE PHYSICISTS, LEÓ SZILÁRD AND EUGENE WIGNER.
WHAT DO THEY WANT?
EINSTEIN! TERRIBLE NEWS!
THE AMERICAN SECRET SERVICE HAVE JUST WARNED US...
THE NAZIS ARE DEVELOPING A POWERFUL NEW BOMB.
AN ATOMIC WEAPON BASED ON THE PRINCIPLES OF YOUR WORK!
AH!
E=MC2... THE EQUATION WHICH DEMONSTRATES THAT ENERGY CAN BE RELEASED FROM MATTER... AND HERE I WAS THINKING THAT IT WOULD NEVER HAVE ANY PRACTICAL USE...
Not like my other ideas, which directly or indirectly were the catalyst for a whole host of applications.
Lasers, GPS, digital cameras, barcode readers, solar panels, CD, DVD...
THE NAZIS ARE MAKING QUICK PROGRESS...
WE MUST ACT! WE MUST INFORM PRESIDENT ROOSEVELT IMMEDIATELY!
WE MUST WARN HIM
2nd August, 1939
Dear Mister President,
The Nazis are working on a powerful new weapon, powered by nuclear fission.
If they succeed, they could destroy the world.

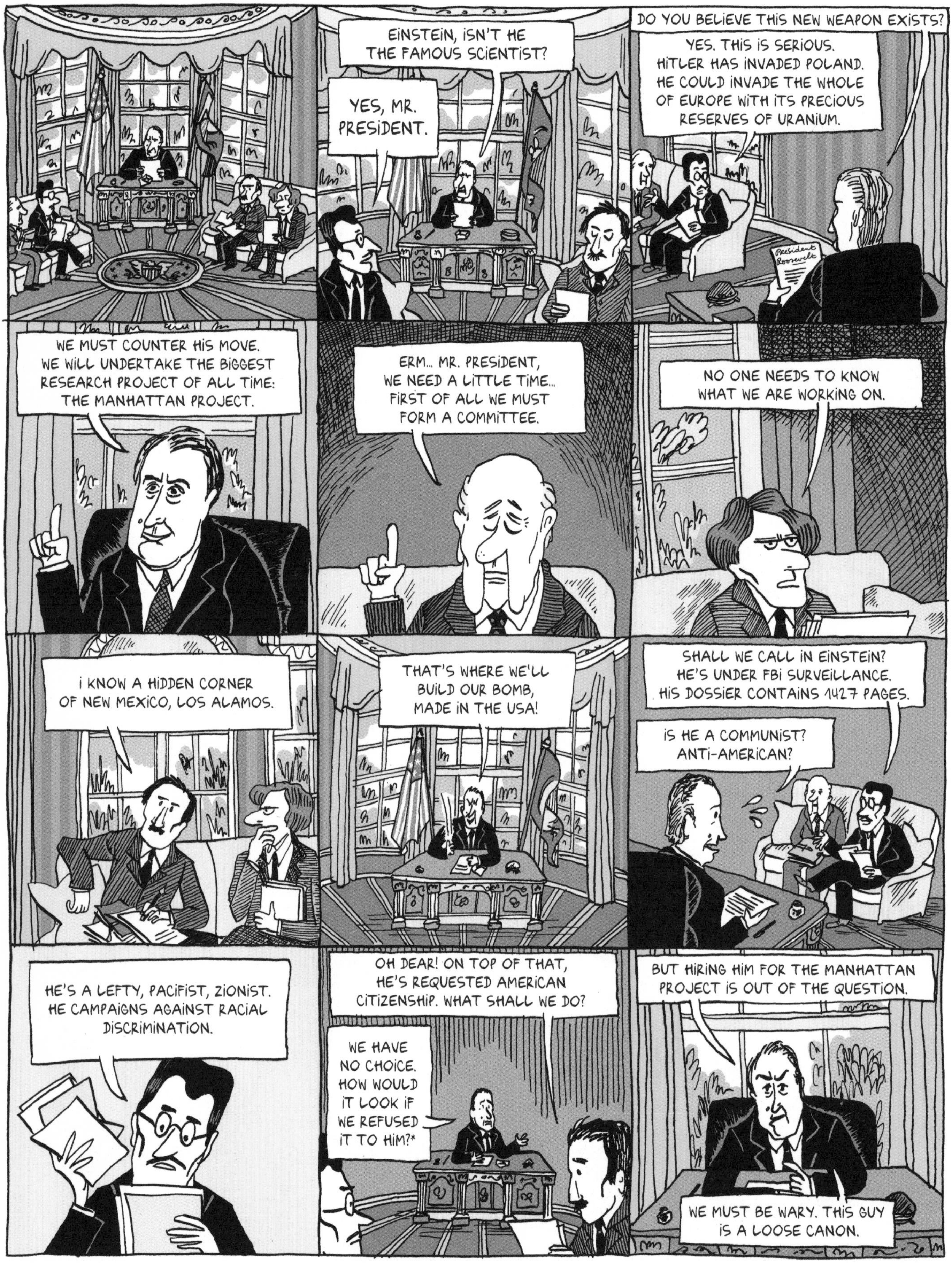
EINSTEIN, ISN'T HE THE FAMOUS SCIENTIST?
YES, MR. PRESIDENT.
DO YOU BELIEVE THIS NEW WEAPON EXISTS?
YES. THIS IS SERIOUS. HITLER HAS INVADED POLAND. HE COULD INVADE THE WHOLE OF EUROPE WITH ITS PRECIOUS RESERVES OF URANIUM.
President Roosevelt
WE MUST COUNTER HIS MOVE. WE WILL UNDERTAKE THE BIGGEST RESEARCH PROJECT OF ALL TIME: THE MANHATTAN PROJECT.
ERM... MR. PRESIDENT, WE NEED A LITTLE TIME... FIRST OF ALL WE MUST FORM A COMMITTEE.
NO ONE NEEDS TO KNOW WHAT WE ARE WORKING ON.
I KNOW A HIDDEN CORNER OF NEW MEXICO, LOS ALAMOS.
THAT'S WHERE WE'LL BUILD OUR BOMB, MADE IN THE USA!
SHALL WE CALL IN EINSTEIN? HE'S UNDER FBI SURVEILLANCE. HIS DOSSIER CONTAINS 1427 PAGES.
IS HE A COMMUNIST? ANTI-AMERICAN?
HE'S A LEFTY, PACIFIST, ZIONIST. HE CAMPAIGNS AGAINST RACIAL DISCRIMINATION.
OH DEAR! ON TOP OF THAT, HE'S REQUESTED AMERICAN CITIZENSHIP. WHAT SHALL WE DO?
WE HAVE NO CHOICE. HOW WOULD IT LOOK IF WE REFUSED IT TO HIM?*
BUT HIRING HIM FOR THE MANHATTAN PROJECT IS OUT OF THE QUESTION.
WE MUST BE WARY. THIS GUY IS A LOOSE CANON.

*Einstein was granted American citizenship in 1940.

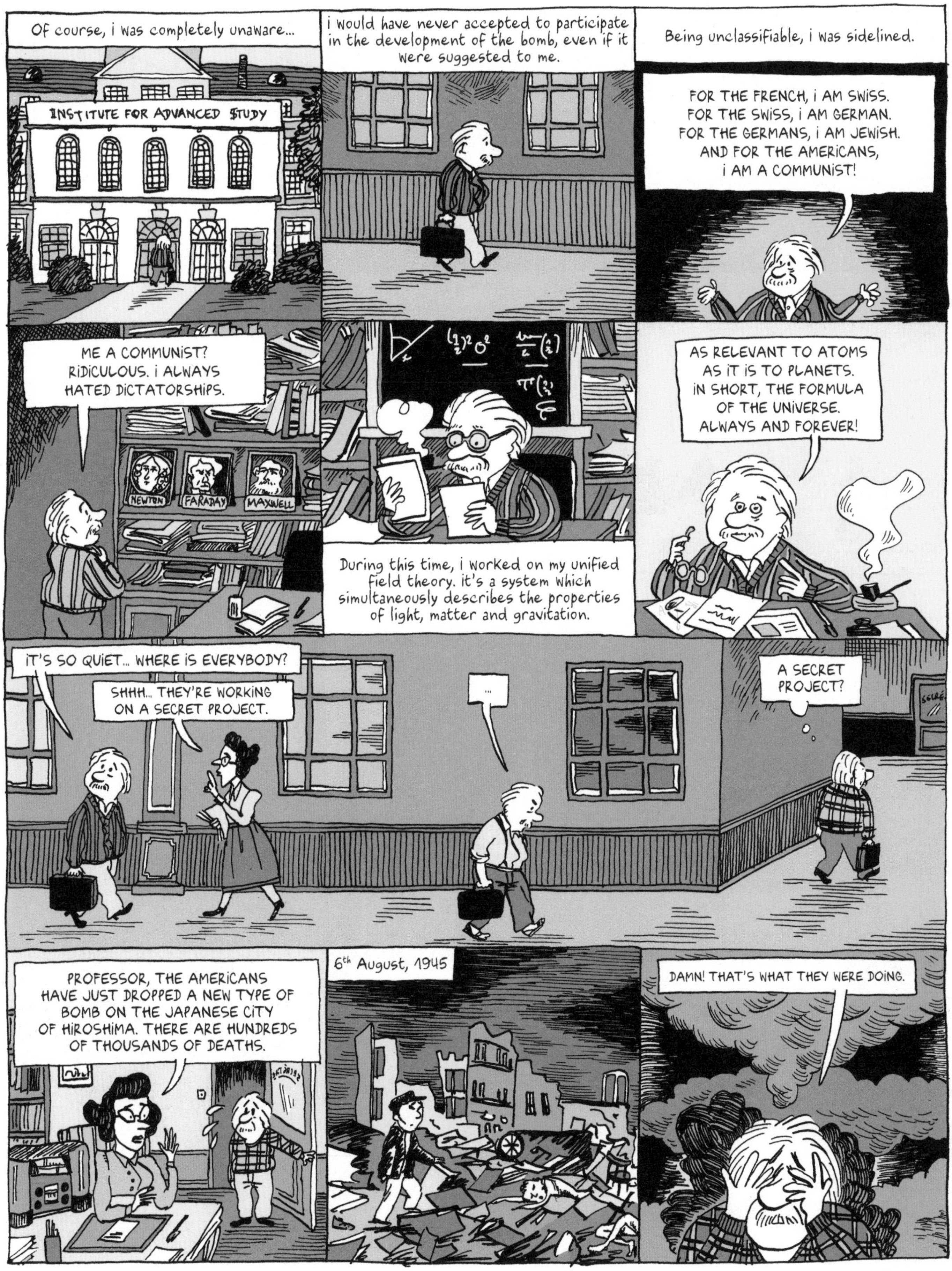
Of course, i was completely unaware...
INSTITUTE FOR ADVANCED STUDY
i would have never accepted to participate in the development of the bomb, even if it were suggested to me.
Being unclassifiable, i was sidelined.
FOR THE FRENCH, i AM SWiSS. FOR THE SWiSS, i AM GERMAN. FOR THE GERMANS, i AM JEWiSH. AND FOR THE AMERiCANS, i AM A COMMUNiST!
ME A COMMUNiST? RiDiCULOUS. i ALWAYS HATED DiCTATORSHiPS.
NEWTON
FARADAY
MAXWELL
During this time, i worked on my unified field theory. it's a system which simultaneously describes the properties of light, matter and gravitation.
AS RELEVANT TO ATOMS AS iT iS TO PLANETS. iN SHORT, THE FORMULA OF THE UNiVERSE. ALWAYS AND FOREVER!
iT'S SO QUiET... WHERE iS EVERYBODY?
SHHH... THEY'RE WORKiNG ON A SECRET PROJECT.
...
A SECRET PROJECT?
PROFESSOR, THE AMERiCANS HAVE JUST DROPPED A NEW TYPE OF BOMB ON THE JAPANESE CiTY OF HiROSHiMA. THERE ARE HUNDREDS OF THOUSANDS OF DEATHS.
6th August, 1945
DAMN! THAT'S WHAT THEY WERE DOiNG.

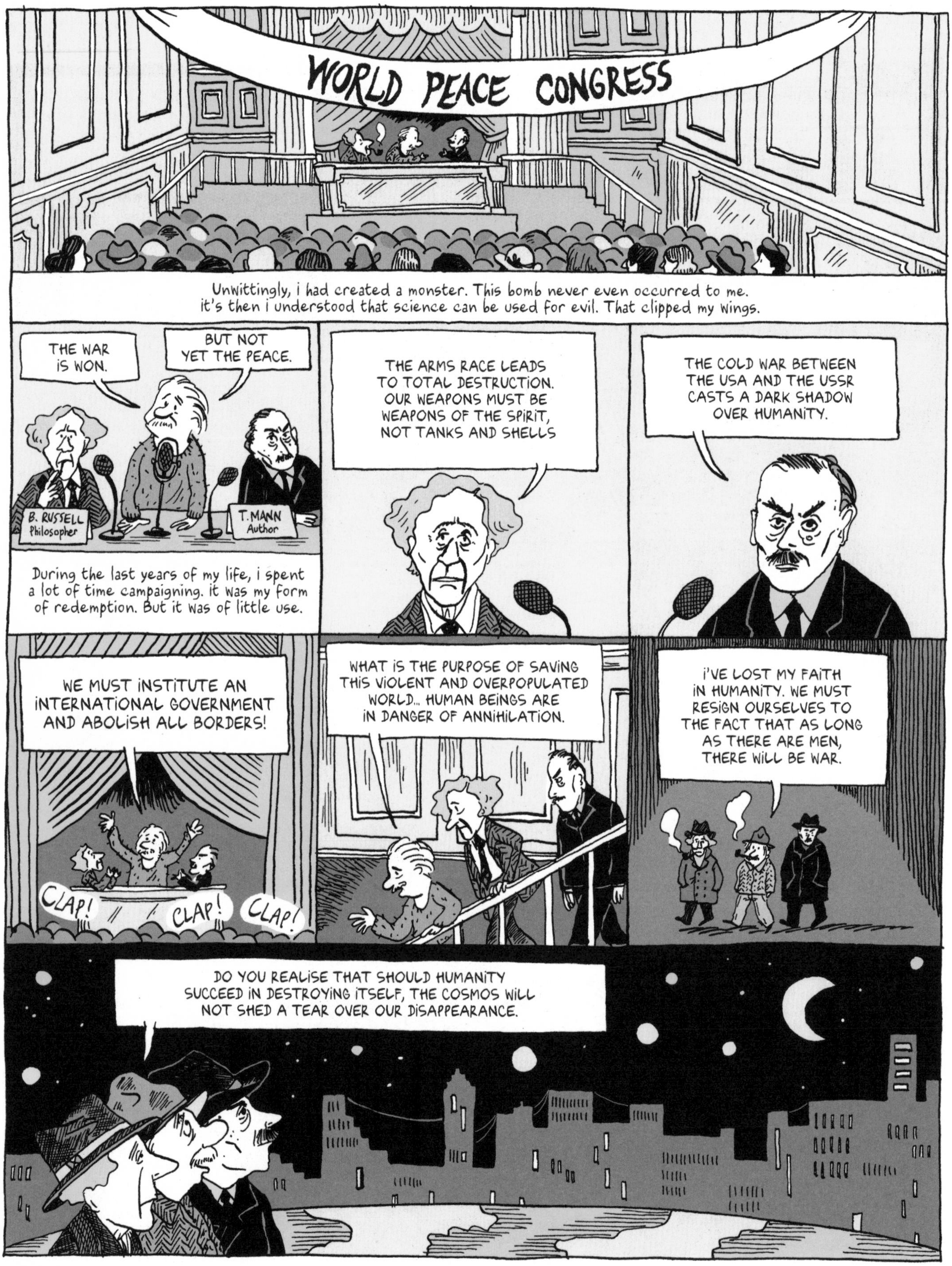
WORLD PEACE CONGRESS
Unwittingly, i had created a monster. This bomb never even occurred to me. it's then i understood that science can be used for evil. That clipped my wings.
THE WAR IS WON.
BUT NOT YET THE PEACE.
B. RUSSELL Philosopher
T. MANN Author
During the last years of my life, i spent a lot of time campaigning. it was my form of redemption. But it was of little use.
THE ARMS RACE LEADS TO TOTAL DESTRUCTION. OUR WEAPONS MUST BE WEAPONS OF THE SPIRIT, NOT TANKS AND SHELLS
THE COLD WAR BETWEEN THE USA AND THE USSR CASTS A DARK SHADOW OVER HUMANITY.
WE MUST INSTITUTE AN INTERNATIONAL GOVERNMENT AND ABOLISH ALL BORDERS!
CLAP! CLAP! CLAP!
WHAT IS THE PURPOSE OF SAVING THIS VIOLENT AND OVERPOPULATED WORLD... HUMAN BEINGS ARE IN DANGER OF ANNIHILATION.
I'VE LOST MY FAITH IN HUMANITY. WE MUST RESIGN OURSELVES TO THE FACT THAT AS LONG AS THERE ARE MEN, THERE WILL BE WAR.
DO YOU REALISE THAT SHOULD HUMANITY SUCCEED IN DESTROYING ITSELF, THE COSMOS WILL NOT SHED A TEAR OVER OUR DISAPPEARANCE.

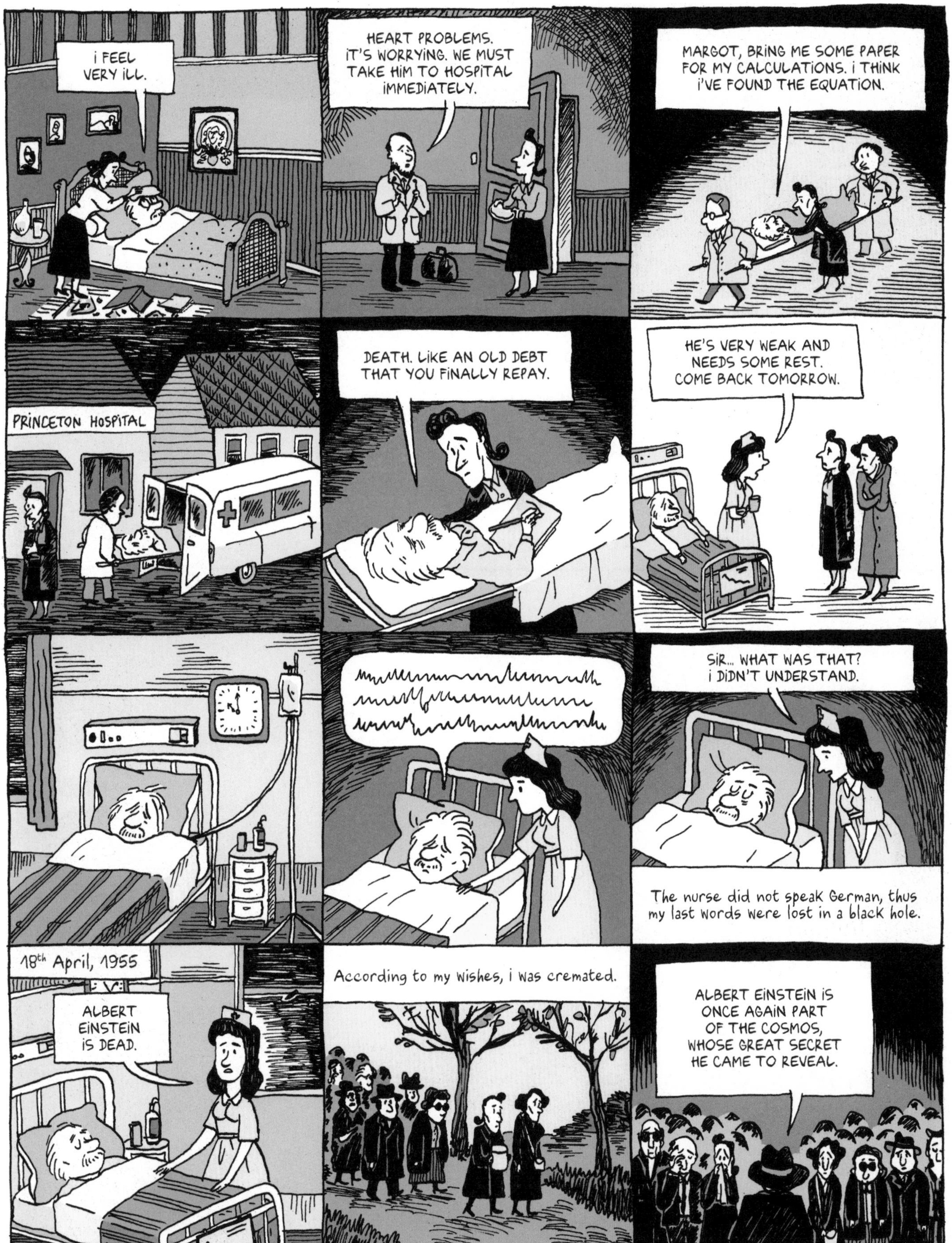
I FEEL VERY ILL.
HEART PROBLEMS. IT'S WORRYING. WE MUST TAKE HIM TO HOSPITAL IMMEDIATELY.
MARGOT, BRING ME SOME PAPER FOR MY CALCULATIONS. I THINK I'VE FOUND THE EQUATION.
PRINCETON HOSPITAL
DEATH. LIKE AN OLD DEBT THAT YOU FINALLY REPAY.
HE'S VERY WEAK AND NEEDS SOME REST. COME BACK TOMORROW.
SIR... WHAT WAS THAT? I DIDN'T UNDERSTAND.
The nurse did not speak German, thus my last words were lost in a black hole.
18th April, 1955
ALBERT EINSTEIN IS DEAD.
According to my wishes, I was cremated.
ALBERT EINSTEIN IS ONCE AGAIN PART OF THE COSMOS, WHOSE GREAT SECRET HE CAME TO REVEAL.

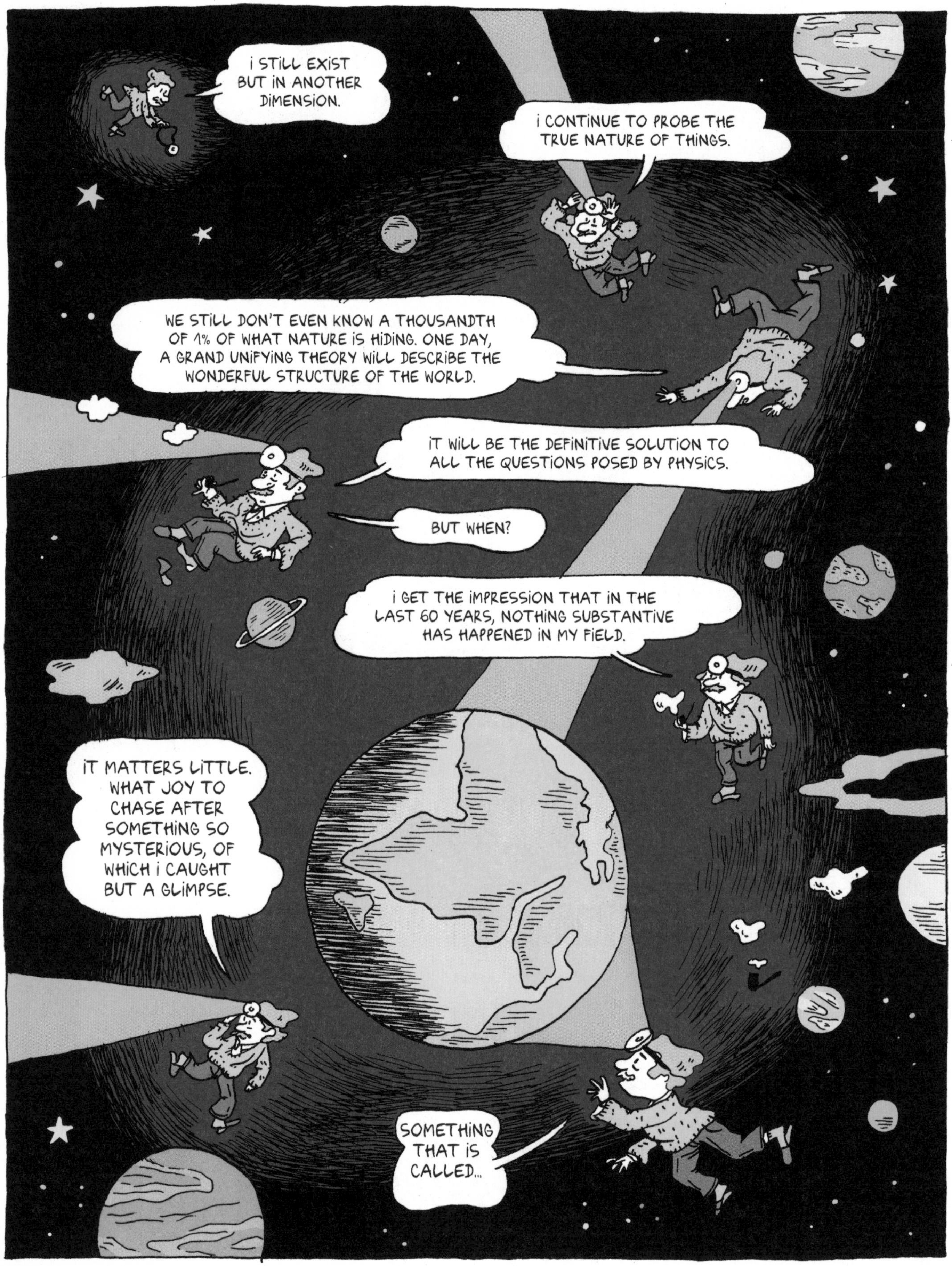
I STILL EXIST BUT IN ANOTHER DIMENSION.
I CONTINUE TO PROBE THE TRUE NATURE OF THINGS.
WE STILL DON'T EVEN KNOW A THOUSANDTH OF 1% OF WHAT NATURE IS HIDING. ONE DAY, A GRAND UNIFYING THEORY WILL DESCRIBE THE WONDERFUL STRUCTURE OF THE WORLD.
IT WILL BE THE DEFINITIVE SOLUTION TO ALL THE QUESTIONS POSED BY PHYSICS.
BUT WHEN?
I GET THE IMPRESSION THAT IN THE LAST 60 YEARS, NOTHING SUBSTANTIVE HAS HAPPENED IN MY FIELD.
IT MATTERS LITTLE. WHAT JOY TO CHASE AFTER SOMETHING SO MYSTERIOUS, OF WHICH I CAUGHT BUT A GLIMPSE.
SOMETHING THAT IS CALLED...

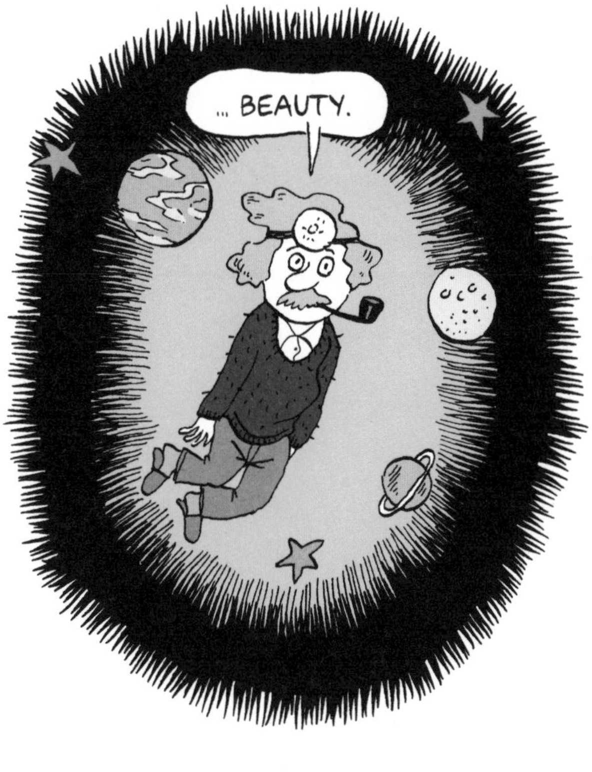
... BEAUTY.

ALSO BY CORINNE MAIER AND ANNE SIMON

FREUD, AN ILLUSTRATED BIOGRAPHY

MARX, AN ILLUSTRATED BIOGRAPHY

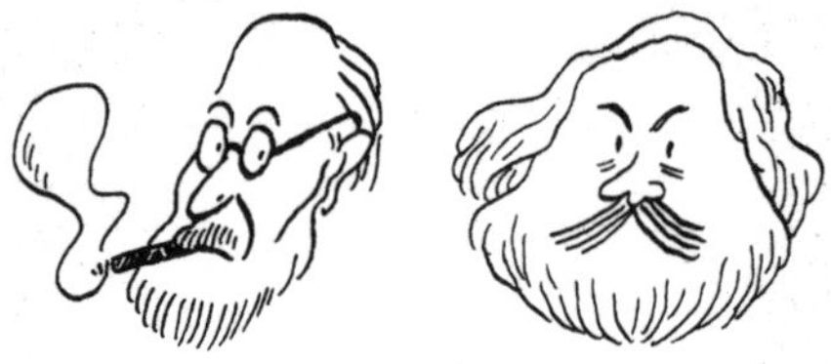